D0996516

America's Urban Capital Stock • Volume One

The Future of

New York City's

Capital Plant

David A. Grossman

An Urban Institute Series

AMERICA'S URBAN CAPITAL STOCK

George E. Peterson
Project Director and Series Editor

This volume is the first in a series of reports on the condition of the nation's urban capital stock and the costs of improving it. Future reports to be published by The Urban Institute will cover the cities of Boston, Cincinnati, Cleveland, Dallas, and Oakland. Other reports in the series will compare capital stock conditions and financing needs for cities in general, and examine the federal policies, if any, that are appropriate in helping cities upgrade their publicly owned capital facilities.

The Future of
New York City's
Capital Plant

This publication reports the results of research sponsored by the Office of Policy Development and Research of the U. S. Department of Housing and Urban Development.

The Future of New York City's Capital Plant

A Case Study of Trends and Prospects Affecting the City's Public Infrastructure

DAVID A. GROSSMAN

The Urban Institute • Washington, D.C.

THE URBAN INSTITUTE is a nonprofit research organization established in 1968 to study problems of the nation's urban communities. Independent and nonpartisan, the Institute responds to current needs for disinterested analyses and basic information and attempts to facilitate the application of this knowledge. As a part of this effort, it cooperates with federal agencies, states, cities, associations of public officials, and other organizations committed to the public interest. The Institute's research findings and a broad range of interpretive viewpoints are published as an educational service.

The work reported in this book was performed under research contract H-2162, Task Order 41 to The Urban Institute through the Office of Policy Development and Research of the U.S. Department of Housing and Urban Development.

The contents of the book reflect the views of the author who is responsible for the facts and accuracy of the data presented. The views expressed do not necessarily reflect those of the United States government in general, the Department of Housing and Urban Development, or The Urban Institute.

Table of Contents

PART 2

PHYSICAL CONDITION OF THE INFRASTRUCTURE

PART 3

FUTURE TRENDS AND PROSPECTS

LIST OF TABLES

LIST OF FIGURES

Foreword

For generations, the publicly owned capital in America's cities has been taken for granted. Whatever other difficulties might beset the cities, it was thought that we could count on the continued delivery of healthful drinking water, the removal of sewage and other wastes, and transportation of city streets and bridges. Indeed, the presence of an in-place infrastructure was thought to confer on old cities one of their few advantages in competing with newer cities for economic development. While growing cities had to launch new capital projects to accommodate their population growth, the older cities had merely to use the capital facilities already at their disposal.

It is now becoming appreciated that preservation of the capital network in good working order requires more vigilance than this. Many of our cities are growing old. Although key elements in the capital system have service lives of 50 years, 100 years, or even longer, many are now reaching the end of their intended use and need to be replaced. The deterioration of the capital plant of older cities is one significant factor in their loss of appeal both for economic enterprises and for more affluent populations.

Maintenance of capital facilities is often a more demanding chore than replacement. Some spectacular failings, such as the collapse of New York City's West Side Highway, have been attributed to maintenance neglect—in this case as simple an omission as failing to paint the elevated supports to prevent rust. Deferred maintenance becomes particularly important in this time of fiscal pressure on city budgets. Because the consequences of postponed maintenance are not immediately visible, maintenance is a tempting candidate for spending cutbacks.

This volume is the first in a series evaluating the capital stock situation in major cities in the United States. Taken together, the several volumes will assess the current condition of urban capital facilities and consider the financial requirements for keeping the stock in satisfactory working order. The series begins with case studies of individual cities. Only at the city level can the complexity of physical captial systems be appreciated, or the constraints imposed by budgetary and other limitations be taken fully into account. And in the end, capital stock preservation is a problem that must be addressed (and to a significant degree, financed) locally.

April 1979   William Gorham
                                                    President

Introduction

This study examines trends and patterns of investment in the physical infrastructure of New York City. It is a "case study" component of a larger survey of urban infrastructure conditions being carried out by The Urban Institute for the U.S. Department of Housing and Urban Development.

The New York City case study is composed of three major parts:

- Part I reviews trends in public spending on the city's capital plant over the last decade and a half.

- Part II examines the physical condition of four key infrastructure systems: water supply and distribution; storm and sanitary sewers; streets and highways; and mass transportation.

- Part III presents the city's estimates of the future needs for capital investment in the infrastructure.

Much of the information used in this study has been provided by New York City agencies, including the Departments of Environmental Protection and Transportation and the New York City Transit Authority. The author wishes to express his deep appreciation to these agencies and to the Office of Management and Budget and the Department of City Planning for their kind cooperation and assistance. However, while acknowledging the very useful assistance that has been provided by these public officials he wants to make it clear that all conclusions and findings as well as any errors of fact or interpretation that the report may contain are the sole responsibility of the author.

Summary

This study of public investment in the physical systems that make up New York City's capital plant reviews the course of capital spending from the mid-sixties to the seventies, explores the present physical condition of the city's major capital systems, and looks toward the city's future capital investment needs and financing capabilities.

Because of the serious financial troubles it has experienced, New York provides an extreme example of the cutbacks in capital investment and maintenance that can result from budgetary pressure on city governments. Between 1974 and 1978, New York's annual capital appropriations fell by nearly 70 percent. Maintenance and repair cycles were stretched—sometimes to extraordinary lengths. Although these spending reductions were part of general budgetary parsimony, capital outlays fell further and more rapidly than did spending on current operations, despite the city's 20 percent reduction in municipal employees. The pressure on the capital budget was particularly acute because New York's temporary default on debt repayments made it impossible to borrow funds for capital spending.

The current condition of the basic systems in the city's physical plant—its water and distribution network, sewers, highways and bridges, and transit—warrant concern, although the systems by and large are managing to perform their designed functions:

Water supply and distribution: A good part of the city's 6,000 miles of water mains is now more than 75 years old and reaching the latter part of its planned life. Coupled with recent reductions in maintenance levels, this has produced a gradual increase in the frequency of main breaks. Physical and fiscal problems have halted construction on the third tunnel bringing water from the Catskill system; without it, neither of the other two tunnels can be shut down for inspection and repair for fear that the by-pass mechanisms will stick shut. *Sewers:* Water pollution treatment plants have been one of the city's biggest capital commitments over the last decade, though outlays have been heavily supported by federal and state aid. Many of the water treatment goals have now been met, and capital spending for this purpose should ease during the next decade. Government priority will shift to maintenance and replacement of existing sewer lines—one of the activities that has experienced sharp cutbacks in spending.

Highways and bridges: The closing and collapse of New York's West Side elevated highway (built in the early 1930s and now being torn down) has become perhaps the archtypical anecdote of urban infrastructure deterioration. Less spectacular but still pronounced are the steep decline in street resurfacing since 1974 and the current "poor" classification of one fourth of the city's waterway bridges. *Transit:* Transit maintenance and replacement programs have fared relatively well compared to other capital categories. Although the city operates aging transit equipment, and estimates that placing its subway system on a 100 year replacement cycle would require nearly doubling present capital outlays, most system performance measures lie within the acceptable range.

In sum, although New York City is not "falling down," its infrastructure is deteriorating and needs a significantly increased rate of investment in maintenance and replacement if serious problems are to be avoided in coming decades. It is a crisis that should be viewed in terms of years or decades—not days or months.

New York's new Ten Year Capital Plan recognizes the urgency of setting out on a coherent plan of capital modernization and repair. The plan calls for a ten year appropriation of $12 billion in city funds plus additional funds for engineering studies. The first four years of this capital program became the cornerstone of the city's request to the President and the Congress for federal loan guarantees to enable the city to sell its securities to its municipal employee pension funds. In effect, federal guarantees have been used to make it possible for the city to finance its plan for capital modernization.

In addition to greatly increasing capital spending levels from their post-crisis levels, the city's capital plan calls for a drastic shift in the functional allocation of capital outlays. The plan represents a back-to-basics movement that would steer funds into streets, bridges, sewer lines, and water distribution systems—while cutting back on capital spending for such politically popular items as education. Now that the city has surmounted its immediate financing problems, it remains to be seen whether it can exercise the political will to redirect its capital priorities to the extent called for in the capital plan. In this, as before in reactions to budgetary strain, New York illustrates (albeit in magnified form) capital investment goals and difficulties common to many of the nation's old and populous cities.

Part 1
Capital Spending Trends

The Financing of Infrastructure Maintenance and Investment

New York City differs from other major American cities more because of its budgetary and financing systems than in the matter of sheer size. To an unusual degree—matched only by Washington and Baltimore—New York has consolidated fiscal responsibility for virtually all major public activities in its municipal budget. For example, activities such as elementary, secondary, and higher education, which are rarely included within city budgets elsewhere, are an integral part of city budgeting and financing in New York. So, too, are the income maintenance and medical assistance programs, water supply, much of the mass transit system, and other activities which elsewhere are more likely to be financed on a county, regional, state, or public authority basis.

For this reason, an examination of the city's budget provides a quite comprehensive overview of the patterns and trends in spending on infrastructure in the five boroughs that make up the city. There are a few exceptions (cited below in the section on "off-budget" financing) but these are fewer than is the case with respect to the central city of most metropolitan regions in the United States.

New York City maintains two separate expenditure budgets: expense and capital. Each is discussed briefly below in terms of its relationship to the infrastructure.

THE EXPENSE BUDGET

New York's expense (or operating) budget, currently at an annual level of $13.5 billion, ranks among the four largest public budgets in the nation.

The principal expenditures provided through the expense budget are, first, the salaries and related expenses of the city's 250,000 employees; second, the cost of income maintenance (welfare) and medical assistance (Medicaid) for the nearly one in eight residents whose incomes make them eligible; and, third, debt service. Together, these activities account for about nine-tenths of the total operating budget of the city.

Since 1976 the city has divided its operating budget into two formal components: the "expense" budget which lists all operating expenditures and the "revenue" budget which lists funds anticipated from city taxes, federal and state operating aid, and other sources. The city's revenues are derived in approximately equal amounts from four sources: real estate taxes; all other city taxes and revenues; federal aid; and state aid.

The city's operating budget has been severely constrained for decades. Annual battles to obtain additional tax revenue or intergovernmental aid have been an unfortunate but continuing aspect of municipal governance in New York. Pressures on the expense budget reached a peak with the onset of the fiscal crisis in the spring of 1975. In the year that followed, the city's work force was cut back by about one-fifth and there has been continuing attrition since that time.

Fiscal pressures have been concentrated on that portion of the city's expense budget (roughly one-half) which is seen as "controllable;" the "uncontrollable" portions include such major items as income maintenance and medical assistance (mandated by state law) and employee pensions and debt service (both mandated by the state constitution).

The portions of the expense budget that relate most directly to the physical infrastructure are staff and contract activities necessary to maintain and operate capital facilities, such as the water supply and distribution system, the sewers and related water pollution control facilities, streets and highways, and the extensive mass transit system. While these maintenance activities are recognized by city officials as crucial to the long run quality of the city's environment, in the short run of fiscal crisis the pressure to cut back spending in those areas has been severe. Data indicating the degree to which these activities have suffered in the fiscal crisis are presented later.

THE CAPITAL BUDGET

New York City's capital budget is legally separate from the expense budget. Since the amendment of the city charter in 1975, however, both budgets have been prepared and adopted concurrently.

Much of the capital budget is devoted to meeting the cost of major facilities and structures, land, and major pieces of equipment, together with the related costs of engineering design and of furnishing. The eligibility of activities for bond financing (capital activities) is defined in the city charter, the state's local finance law and regulations issued by the state comptroller.

An unusual aspect of the city's capital budget arises from the fact that for decades preceding the fiscal crisis of 1975 New York City took advantage of provisions of state legislation to include in its capital budget appropriations which in strict municipal accounting parlance would be defined as operating costs. In the several years preceding 1975 this practice expanded rapidly, spurred by the severe fiscal burden on the expense budget. By fiscal 1975* more than half of all city funds available for the capital budget were allocated to operating costs. One result was to force a reduction in the city's ability to invest in its infrastructure and related capital facilities even before the fiscal crisis, which struck in March, 1975 (further discussed below), required even sharper cutbacks.

The state constitution provides the basic framework for financing the city's capital budget. It does so through provisions related to the debt limit, debt service, and the duration of debt.

The Debt Limit • The state constitution limits the amount of long-term debt outstanding for capital purposes to not more than 10 percent of the equalized value of taxable real property in the city (averaged over five years). A related provision allows debt for low and moderate income housing to be issued in amounts of not more than 2 percent of total assessed value. The major exceptions to these limits, as spelled out in the constitution are: water supply; water pollution control; and self-supporting projects such as parking garages and public markets.

At present the constitutional debt limit is about $8 billion. This is not currently a major constraint on city capital budgeting nor does it appear likely to become one within the next five or so years, because

---

* New York City's fiscal year runs from July 1 to June 30. Fiscal 1975 refers to the year which began on July 1, 1974 and ended on June 30, 1975.

of the presence of other constraints on the city's ability to borrow
and spend for capital projects.

Debt Service • The city is authorized by the state constitution
to levy real estate taxes without limit to pay for debt service on long-
term debt. This open-ended provision contrasts sharply with the
limitation on the annual levy of real estate taxes for operating purposes (2.5 percent of equalized valuation).

Length of Debt • The constitution and related state law also
sets forth a framework for the term of bonds that can be issued for
various capital purposes. These "periods of probable usefulness" are
a constraint (but not a very limiting one) on the city's capital program. In past years New York's long-term debt structure was characterized by relatively short maturities (by choice as much as by
constitutional constraint).

The most severe fiscal limitation on New York's capital program
since March, 1975, has been the public market for municipal securities rather than any provisions of the state constitution or state law.
The effective exclusion of the city from the long-term municipal
security market since early 1975 has forced New York to look to
other sources to finance its capital program. The only substantial
source that has been available (apart from direct federal and state
grants-in-aid) has been the purchase of city bonds by the municipal
employee pension funds.

OFF-BUDGET CAPITAL FINANCING

In addition to the capital financing available through the city's
budgets, some components of the infrastructure have also been addressed by state, multi-state, and even federal agencies.

Several agencies of New York State have assumed infrastructure
responsibilities within the city:

The Metropolitan Transportation Authority is a state agency
which controls the New York City Transit Authority and the
Triborough Bridge and Tunnel Authority. The Transit Authority's capital program, however, is financed through the city's
capital budget; Triborough is self-supporting through tolls.

The state has a parks agency which directly builds and finances selected facilities within the city.

State housing and development authorities such as the

Battery Park City Authority and the Urban Development Corporation operate within the city's limits.

The State Facilities Corporation has built a number of hospital facilities for the city. These have received long-term financing through a state "moral obligation" agency but with all debt service paid by the city.

The State Dormitory Authority builds facilities for City University which are financed by "moral obligation" debt issued by the Authority and paid for in equal shares by the city and the state.

The bi-state Port Authority, authorized under an interstate compact, has financed and built a major system of bridges and tunnels between New York and New Jersey as well as the regional airports and port facilities. Its financing comes from tolls and rentals.

In several instances, federal agencies have undertaken direct responsibility for infrastructure components located within the city. The National Parks Service operates the bi-state Gateway National Park located on both sides of the entrance to New York harbor. The U.S. Army Corps of Engineers has planned storm damage prevention facilities along the city's ocean front and recently completed an important study of water supply and distribution needs of the city and the surrounding region.

IMPACT OF THE FISCAL CRISIS

While there are differing views as to the causes of New York City's fiscal crisis, what happened in its immediate aftermath is pretty much a matter of record. The city's issuances of short- and long-term securities began to experience difficulties toward the end of 1974. The initial signs of trouble were rapid rises in the interest rates required by the investment syndicates which were the customary first-instance purchasers of city securities. The city attempted to meet the problem by various techniques (such as revising its issuance schedule) but after March, 1975, the city became unable to sell any of its own securities on the open market.

When the market closed to the city, New York lost two vital fund sources: the capital budget was almost totally dependent on sales of long-term bonds and the expense budget had become heavily dependent both on sales of short-term securities and on sales of long-term bonds to finance the operating activities appropriated for in the capital budget.

Attempts by the city to replace the public securities market's role took on a number of forms in the months and years after the onset of the fiscal crisis. These included negotiated sales of long-term securities to municipal employee pension funds, reliance on a newly created state agency (the Municipal Assistance Corporation) which sold "moral obligation" securities backed by claims on city revenues and state aid, and loans from the federal and state governments. In addition, the city cut back sharply on both capital and expense budget spending to reduce its revenue needs.

While the city has recently achieved a modest return to the public securities market (it has sold several issues of short-term notes in 1979), the general securities market has remained closed to the city since 1975. This has had marked effects on both city budgets.

Impact on the Capital Budget • Beginning in 1975, the capital budget became dependent on a three year agreement negotiated between the city and the trustees of the municipal employee pension funds under which about one billion dollars per year in long-term city securities were placed with the pension funds. Only about half of this resource was available for "true" capital projects because of a phenomenon mentioned above: the use of capital funds to finance growing portions of the operating budget. The remaining half of the $3 billion made available by pension fund purchase of city securities had to be allocated to operating program needs in fiscal years 1976 to 1978 (the "first financial plan" period).

The city initiated a massive cutback of its capital program in 1975. Partially completed structures were stopped in mid-construction, plans ready for bidding were put on the shelf and the design program ground to a halt. The only major capital projects that continued to advance were those that were wholly funded by intergovernmental grants or those where there was an unbreakable commitment to move ahead (as in the case of transit projects to which the city was committed under special provisions of federal legislation).

The effects of the cutback were sharp: total construction contracts awarded fell from annual levels of over $700 million in fiscal years 1974 and 1975 to $300 million or less in fiscal years 1976 and 1977. Most of the construction awards in the three "first plan" years of 1976 to 1978 were financed by federal and state grants or represented matching commitments made by the city to obtain such grants. Without them, construction awards in these three years would have been virtually nil.

Impact on the Expense Budget • Severe cutbacks in the expense budget paralleled the near-stoppage of the capital program but were not as precipitous because of the nature of the essential services provided by the operating budget. The roughly half of the city's expense budget that is "uncontrollable" because it is mandated by the state constitution or state law could not be reduced significantly. Of necessity, the remainder of the expense budget was reduced sharply, and the city's work force was reduced by about one-fifth through a combination of layoffs and attrition.

Among the operating activities that were hard hit in the budget cuts of the fiscal 1975 to 1978 period were programs for maintaining the physical infrastructure. Repair and maintenance activities by city staffs and contractors were both cut back severely. Later in this study, these cuts are outlined in more detail.

PROSPECTS FOR THE NEAR FUTURE

With the start of the Koch Administration in 1978, the city entered a four year "second financial plan" period. During this period the capital program will continue to rely heavily on purchases of long-term bonds by the municipal employee pension funds (substantially backed by federal guarantees signed into law by President Carter in August, 1978). The amount of city funding and aid appears to be sufficient to allow a substantial increase above crisis period spending levels on the capital program and especially on the infrastructure components of that program. However, the city's expense budget will continue to be under extreme pressure and further reductions in the city's work force, primarily by attrition, are anticipated; the plan currently calls for a work force reduction of 12 percent over the fiscal years 1980 to 1982.

During the "second plan" period the city expects to complete the phasing-out of capital funds as a source of revenue for the operating budget (now scheduled to end prior to fiscal 1982). The outstanding short-term debt left from the fiscal crisis period will be funded over a longer period, primarily through issuance of securities by the Municipal Assistance Corporation with debt service to be paid by the city.

The city's plans currently call for a general return to the public securities markets by about fiscal 1982, the date by which the operating budget will be fully balanced in terms of generally accepted accounting principles.

Capital
Budget
Appropriations

In the thirteen years from fiscal 1966 to 1979, New York City appropriated a total of nearly $16.5 billion in its annual capital budgets. Of this amount, two-thirds were city funds; the remainder was anticipated federal and state grants for capital projects.

Here we will examine the thirteen year pattern of city capital appropriations in terms of overall trends, the functional aspects of city activities toward which the appropriations were directed, and the sources of funds involved. Prior to that examination, however, a cautionary note is presented describing key aspects of capital budget practice in New York City to provide the reader a better basis for understanding the data and the patterns they present.

CAPITAL BUDGET PRACTICES

In examining data from New York City's capital budget in the fiscal years from 1966 to 1979, the reader should be cognizant of a number of practices followed by the city, including some that have changed during the period. Among the most significant practices and changes that have taken place in them, are the following:

Appropriations • The city's capital budget is an appropriating document; once an item has been approved, funds can be spent for it (as contrasted to the capital budget in the years prior to 1965 when an authorization practice was also used). Once appropriated, capital funds are generally available until spent or rescinded.

11

Sequential Appropriation • Typically, the city's capital budget includes funds for a particular project in sequential stages: site acquisition, design, construction, and furnishing/equipment. In some cases, construction appropriations may themselves be staged.

Time Lags • There are frequently time lags of one, two, or more years between appropriation and expenditure of capital funds. There often are further time lags between expenditures and the issuance of bonds to finance a particular capital project.

State and Federal Funds • Prior to the fiscal 1976 budget, intergovernmental aid (state and federal funds) was not appropriated by the Board of Estimate and the City Council but was made available for expenditure by unilateral action of the mayor. The budget bureau generally tried to keep the stated amounts of such aid close to what was realistically anticipated but the practice was less tightly followed than it was for city funds in the pre-1976 period.

Amendment • The capital budget can be amended after its adoption to increase the amount of funds available; in fact, the charter has generally allowed the mayor himself to increase the amount of any appropriation by up to 15 percent (to account for escalating costs). During some years of heavy construction awards and rapid cost escalation (fiscal years 1970 to 1973 in particular) amendments added up to $100 million in city funds in some years. These amounts are not included in the appropriations data; however, it is the author's judgment that if they were they would not change the trends discussed in significant ways.

Rescindment • Capital funds not needed for a particular project (i.e., left over after its completion) can be rescinded. In addition, unexpended appropriations can be rescinded to make room within the constitutional debt limit for other projects. There were $25 million or more in rescindments in most of the years from 1966 to 1979; and in some years at the height of the fiscal crisis (1975 to 1978) the rescindments were even larger. Generally, these rescindments applied only to city debt limit appropriations. These amounts are not included in the appropriations data; as in the previous case, it is the author's judgment that the omission does not significantly affect overall trends.

Operating Funds • Throughout the period 1966–79, New York City utilized portions of its capital budget for activities generally defined in accounting standards as operating purposes. The major items that fell in this category were funds for manpower training and vocational education, code enforcement, repair programs, purchase of motor vehicles smaller than trucks, and lease payments.

During fiscal years 1976 to 1979 these funds were separately identified in the capital budgets and have not been included in the appropriations data. Prior to that time, amounts ranging from $25 to $100 million per year were included in the data because it was so difficult to identify them. A substantial part of the funds of this type in fiscal year 1975 and earlier were included in the human resources and housing categories; relatively small amounts were included in the water, sewer, highways, or transit categories.

Off-Budget Appropriations • New York City has made use of a number of city and state authorities to finance different aspects of its capital program. For example: (a) after fiscal 1966 much of the senior college construction program and after about 1971 much of the community college construction program was financed through the City University Construction Fund and the New York State Dormitory Authority; and (b) after about 1969 much of the hospital construction program was financed through the New York State Housing Finance Agency.

These appropriations generally did not appear in the capital budget but involved substantial amounts of construction during the 1966–1979 period. These amounts *are* included in the section on capital program expenditures, which examines construction contract awards.

Housing • Changes in federal policy with respect to urban renewal (from Title I of the Housing Act of 1949 to the neighborhood renewal program to the Community Development Program) were reflected in successive changes in city budgeting practices. After 1968 and until 1974 anticipated federal grant funds were shown in the capital budget. With the inception of the Community Development Block Grant Program this practice was no longer followed. In addition, the "executive" category in the capital budget included major amounts for the city share of the Model Cities program from 1968 to about 1975.

Organization • Numerous changes in city agency structure and responsibility occurred in the period 1966–79. Where feasible, the changes have been adjusted to keep the data for a function consistent from one year to the next. These changes have not been separately footnoted; to do so would virtually require the writing of a history of administrative change in the city for the period.

The net result of these practices is that data on New York City capital budget appropriations must be used with some caution. Precise comparability over time between and within functional categories and by source of funds is very difficult (in fact, probably impossible) to achieve. The problems are especially acute in the following functional categories for which data is presented in Table 2 below:

- Economic Development
- Higher Education
- Executive

- Health and Hospitals
- Housing
- Human Resources

Most of the other functional categories of the capital budget have followed reasonably consistent budgeting practices. These include the four categories which are the particular focus of this case study (water, sewers, highways, and transit), but even in these cases there are minor effects due to changes in budgetary practice.

Despite the drawbacks cited above, there is good reason for believing that the data on New York's capital budget appropriations presented in this study represent a useful and reasonably accurate description of the city's principal capital program decisions in the 1966–79 period. First, the allocations for most functions are generally good reflections of the construction program (as can be seen in a comparison with actual construction awards in the same period: see pages 29ff.). Second, the allocations by sources of funds are also generally accurate reflections of reality (for example, with respect to the concentration of state and federal grants in particular functional categories).

TRENDS IN TOTAL APPROPRIATIONS

Table 1 and figure 1 present a summary of annual appropriations by major fund source. All data in the tables in this text are on the basis of actual appropriation data, not adjusted for inflation; therefore, changes in amounts from year to year must be viewed with caution. Even on an unadjusted basis, however, it seems clear that

Table 1

SUMMARY OF NEW YORK CITY CAPITAL BUDGET APPROPRIATIONS BY SOURCE OF FUNDS, FISCAL YEARS 1966–79

(in $ millions)

Fiscal Year	Total All Funds	Total, City Sources	City Debt Limit	City Outside Limit	Total, S & F Sources	Federal Funds	State Funds
1979	1,004.2	541.9	477.3	94.6	462.3	436.6	25.7
1978	695.5	228.6	195.1	33.5	466.9	318.3	148.6
1977	1,188.9	437.1	376.4	60.7	751.8	568.2	183.6
1976	1,545.5	988.9	756.3	232.6	556.1	319.7	236.4
1975	1,371.9	997.3	852.9	144.4	374.6	321.7	52.9
1974	2,233.4	1,320.5	1,122.6	197.9	902.9	778.4	124.5
1973	1,808.9	1,302.7	997.2	305.5	506.2	224.4	281.8
1972	1,568.4	1,124.3	807.3	317.0	444.1	104.1	340.0
1971	1,213.7	935.7	750.0	185.7	278.0	74.5	203.5
1970	1,077.3	790.4	719.1	71.4	286.8	132.1	152.7
1969	719.3	570.1	491.9	78.2	149.2	59.0	90.2
1968	817.5	611.6	536.1	75.5	205.9	58.8	147.1
1967	650.4	532.1	432.2	99.9	118.3	13.2	105.1
1966	587.4	583.8	496.6	87.2	3.6	1.1	2.5
Total 1966–79	16,482.3	10,964.9	8,981.0	1,983.9	5,506.7	3,410.1	2,096.6

SOURCE: New York City Capital Budgets, 1966–79.

FIGURE 1.
NEW YORK CITY CAPITAL BUDGET APPROPRIATIONS,
FISCAL YEARS 1966-1979.

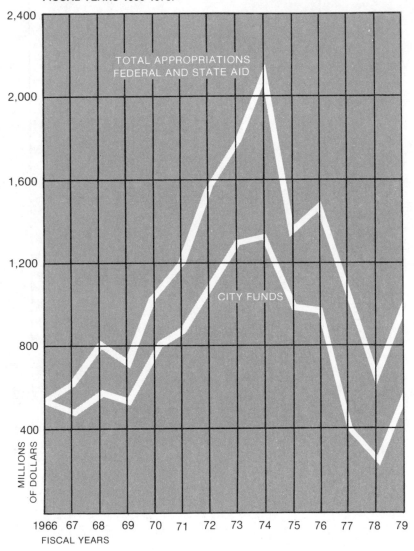

the city's capital budget grew significantly in most years from fiscal 1966 to 1974.

The decline in budgetary appropriations that began in fiscal 1975 pre-dated the fiscal crisis that struck halfway through that year. The cutback from 1974 to 1975 was largely due to a rapid rise in the use of capital funds for operating purposes in 1973 and 1974 which left the city with less capacity to appropriate funds for "true" capital projects that were chargeable to the constitutional debt limit; it was also because city budgeting practices beginning in fiscal 1975 made it possible to exclude capital funds appropriated for operating purposes from the totals in the table. Unfortunately, it is not possible on the basis of available data to recalculate appropriations prior to fiscal 1975 on a fully comparable basis; however, the author estimates that the fiscal 1974 data includes about $100 million in such funds and that there were lesser amounts in earlier years, trending back to about $25 million in fiscal 1966.*

A 12 percent increase in total capital budget funds occurred from 1975 to 1976, primarily because of a gain in state aid; city funds remained at essentially the same level. The impact of the fiscal crisis can be seen most clearly in sharp drops in total appropriations of 23 percent in 1977 and 42 percent in 1978.

In the budget for fiscal 1979 the city began to anticipate the effect that federal guarantees of long term bonds would have on its ability to expand its capital program. Total appropriations grew by 44 percent. Even this level, however, was well below the unadjusted capital budget level of any precrisis fiscal year dating back to 1969. And on an inflation-adjusted basis, it would appear that the fiscal 1979 budget is only about at (or may even be below) the appropriation level of the city in 1966.

TRENDS BY FUNCTIONAL CATEGORIES

Table 2 summarizes capital budget appropriations by 25 functional categories for the period 1966 to 1979. For the most part, these functional categories correspond to city agencies or identifiable components of agencies. The categories in the capital budget have remained relatively constant even though there have been a number

---

* These estimates are lower than the amounts of capital funds actually used for operating purposes in the fiscal years 1966 to 1974 because significant amounts of such funds were appropriated through a mayoral certification process, rather than through the city's capital budget.

of major reorganizations (mergers, splits, transfers, etc.) of city agencies since 1966; in several cases, however, items have been reclassified on the basis of the author's experience to keep them in the same functional category as they are at present (fiscal 1979).

Table 2

SUMMARY OF TOTAL CAPITAL BUDGET APPROPRIATIONS BY MAJOR FUNCTIONAL CATEGORIES, FISCAL YEARS 1966–79

Category	Total Appropriations 1966–79 ($ millions)	Percent of Total
Economic Development	468.7	2.9
Education	2,515.7	15.3
Higher Education	318.7	1.9
Pollution Control Plants	2,966.4	18.1
Sewers	691.3	4.2
Water Mains	256.9	1.6
Sanitation	432.5	2.6
Water Supply	212.2	1.3
Executive	325.1	2.0
Health and Hospitals	576.1	3.5
Housing	962.9	5.8
Human Resources	311.4	1.9
General Services	495.2	3.0
Libraries	99.9	0.6
Museums and Institutions	71.8	0.4
Parks	423.6	2.6
Correction	103.8	0.6
Fire	158.9	1.0
Police	157.5	1.0
Courts	82.3	0.5
Ferries and Airports	69.0	0.4
Highways	673.0	4.1
Waterway Bridges	54.4	0.3
Traffic	187.3	1.1
Transit	3,818.2	23.2
TOTAL	16,482.3	100.0

NOTE: Items may not add to total because of rounding.
SOURCE: New York City Capital Budgets, 1966–79.

As can be seen in table 2, of the 25 categories three together accounted for nearly 57 cents out of every capital dollar appropriated during the thirteen year period. Taking the three singly, transit alone accounted for 23 percent, water pollution control plants for 18 percent, and education for 15 percent.

The infrastructure elements on which attention will be focused in part II of this study accounted for over half of the thirteen year appropriation. This was made up as follows:

	Appropriations Fiscal 1966–79 ($ millions)	Percent of Total City Appropriations
Water Supply and Mains	$ 469	3%
Water Pollution Control:		
Treatment Plants	2,966	18
Sewers	691	4
Highways and Waterway Bridges	727	4
Transit	3,818	23
Subtotal, above items	$ 8,672	53

SELECTED INFRASTRUCTURE TRENDS

Figure 2 shows trends over time of the capital budget appropriations for the principal infrastructure categories selected for focus in this analysis: water; pollution control and sewers; highways and bridges; and transit.

Throughout each of the past thirteen years the transit construction program and the treatment plant portion of the pollution control construction program have been significantly larger than the other selected components (water, sewers, and highways and bridges). This has been especially true since the early 1970s when major amounts of federal and state aid for transit and treatment plant construction began to become available to the city. Primarily for this reason, transit and treatment plant construction were the only ones of the selected categories which resisted the fiscal crisis that affected the 1976 to 1978 capital budgets.

The other selected categories (water, sewers, and highways and bridges) followed roughly parallel appropriation trends over the thirteen years. All demonstrated very flat trends in dollar appropriations until about 1970, followed by gradual upturns until about 1976 when the trend was sharply reversed by the fiscal crisis. The fiscal

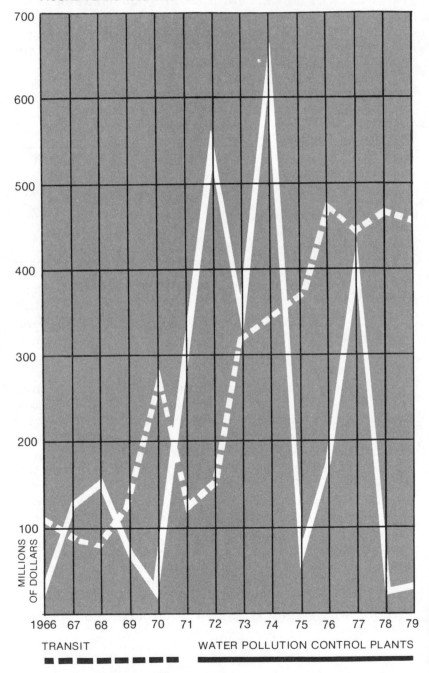

FIGURE 2.
CAPITAL BUDGET APPROPRIATIONS
FOR SELECTED CATEGORIES,
FISCAL YEARS 1966-1979.

MILLIONS OF DOLLARS

TRANSIT

WATER POLLUTION CONTROL PLANTS

FIGURE 2.

CAPITAL BUDGET APPROPRIATIONS FOR SELECTED CATEGORIES, FISCAL YEARS 1966-1979.

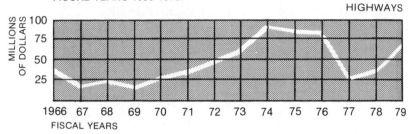

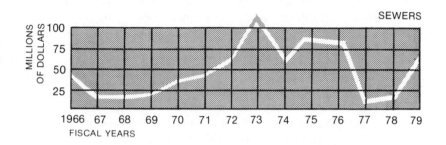

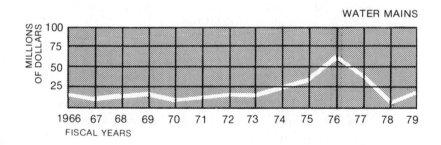

1979 budget resumed growth in appropriations for water, sewers, and highways and bridges. As will subsequently be noted in some detail, the city's capital program forecasts a continuing upswing in these three infrastructure categories during the next decade.

TRENDS BY SOURCE OF FUNDS

New York City's capital budget relies on four principal sources of funds (see table 3):

- City capital funds within the constitutional debt limit are derived from borrowing and are subject to the overall limit of 10 percent of the equalized value of taxable real property outstanding at any time. Debt limit funds are used to finance all capital projects except those eligible for one of the other three fund sources.

- City capital funds can be borrowed *outside* the debt limit for water supply and distribution, water pollution control (including sanitary but not storm sewers), and revenue-generating projects (to the extent that the revenues meet at least one-quarter of annual debt service). At times in the past there have been other debt limit exemptions (e.g., transit and hospitals), but such funds have been available in only miniscule amounts since fiscal 1966.

- Federal capital aid has been available primarily for transit, water pollution control, and urban renewal.

- State aid for the city's capital program has been derived from periodic bond issues (after state-wide referenda) and has been concentrated in water pollution control, transit, and higher education.

In addition to these four major sources of capital funds there have been a variety of other sources, all of them quite small in relation to the size of the capital budget. Private funds to match city contributions are most common in the construction programs of the city-aided museums and cultural institutions. At times, surplus funds from the Triborough Bridge and Tunnel Authority have been made available for the city's capital program, as have revenues from the sale of various capital assets (e.g., the Transit Authority's electric generating plants, which were sold to the Consolidated Edison Company prior to fiscal 1966).

Table 3

SHARES OF TOTAL CAPITAL BUDGET APPROPRIATIONS BY SOURCE OF FUNDS, FISCAL YEARS 1966–79

Fiscal Year	City Funds			Intergovernmental Aid		
	Total City Sources	City Debt Limit	City Exempt Funds	Total Aid	Federal Aid	State Aid
1979	54.0	44.5	9.4	46.0	43.5	2.5
1978	32.9	28.1	4.8	67.1	45.8	21.4
1977	36.8	31.7	5.1	63.2	47.8	15.4
1976	64.0	48.9	15.1	36.0	20.7	15.3
1975	72.7	62.2	10.5	27.3	23.4	3.9
1974	59.1	50.3	8.9	40.4	34.9	5.6
1973	72.0	55.1	16.8	28.0	12.4	15.6
1972	71.7	51.5	20.2	28.3	6.6	21.7
1971	77.1	61.8	15.3	22.9	6.1	16.8
1970	73.4	66.8	6.6	26.6	12.3	14.4
1969	79.3	68.4	10.9	20.7	8.2	12.5
1968	74.8	65.6	9.2	25.2	7.2	18.0
1967	81.8	66.5	15.4	18.2	2.0	16.2
1966	99.4	84.5	14.8	0.6	0.2	0.4
Total 1966–79	66.5	54.4	12.0	33.4	20.7	12.7

SOURCE: Calculated from table 1 above (data from New York City Capital Budgets, 1966–79).

As noted above, some city capital projects (most notably, City University structures and hospitals) have been financed by state agency bond issuances, with the debt service being paid by the city. These appropriations have generally not been included in the capital budget.

In brief, the relative amounts of appropriations from different fund sources from 1966 to 1979 have been as follows:

	Amount ($ millions)	Percent of total
City funds	$ 10,965	67 percent
Federal funds	3,410	21
State funds	2,097	13
Total, all funds	$ 16,472	100 percent

Intergovernmental Aid • Over the 1966–79 period, federal capital aid has tended to rise on an almost unbroken trend while state aid has been both lower and much more variable. One should not, however, attribute much importance to one or two year variations in these data. Given the project-based nature of the capital budget, the amount of aid budgeted by the city in a given year is at least as dependent on the progress of engineering design work on particular projects as it is on the legal provisions governing federal and state capital aid.

The distribution of federal and state grants has followed a strikingly different pattern from the overall distribution of city capital appropriations.

Over 90 percent of all federal grants* were concentrated in only three functional categories: transit, water pollution control plants, and housing (see table 4, part 1). Of these, the housing category cannot be relied on for analytic purposes (as noted elsewhere in this report) because of the great variations in the way the city has treated federal aid as the characteristics of federal legislation and regulations changed.

Over 90 percent of state aid also was concentrated in three categories: water pollution control plants, transit and higher education (see table 4, part 2). State aid in the higher education category is not accurately reflected by city budget figures because of the establishment in 1966 of the City University Construction Fund (which has meant that most of CUNY's construction program was treated in an "off-budget" fashion).

Thus, for capital budget purposes intergovernmental aid has been highly concentrated in a few functional categories. Transit and water pollution control plants, the dominant categories in both fed-

---

* In addition to specific categorical grants for capital construction, the federal government also provides New York City with aid under three general-purpose programs which can be—and in some cases, have been—used for capital construction:

General Revenue Sharing is available for capital construction but has not been so used in New York City. The severe pressures on the city's operating budget have led to all federal revenue-sharing funds being used for operations.

Community Development Block Grants (CDBG) have been used in part for capital projects as well as housing programs. Up to 1979, most CDBG funds were used for housing improvement and maintenance; to the degree that they were used for capital projects, they would be accounted for in the functional area of any specific project that is so aided.

Local Public Works. These funds were used for a variety of capital projects from 1976 to 1978 and were budgeted by the city in connection with specific projects to be aided.

Table 4

FEDERAL AND STATE AID IN THE CAPITAL BUDGET,
SELECTED CATEGORIES, FISCAL YEARS 1966–79

Category	Amount ($ millions)	Percent of Total
Federal Aid		
Transit	1,577.0	46.2
Pollution Control Plants	1,114.5	32.7
Housing	463.8	13.6
All Other Categories	254.8	7.5
Total Federal Aid	3,410.1	100.0
State Aid		
Transit	710.8	33.9
Pollution Control Plants	1,105.9	52.7
Higher Education	110.5	5.3
All Other Categories	169.4	8.1
Total State Aid	2,096.6	100.0
Total Intergovernmental Aid		
Transit	2,287.8	41.5
Pollution Control Plants	2,220.4	40.3
Housing	463.8	8.4
Higher Education	115.5	2.1
All Other Categories	419.2	7.6
Total Aid	5,506.7	100.0

SOURCE: New York City Capital Budgets, 1966–79.

eral and state aid, each accounted for just over 40 percent of all intergovernmental aid in the last thirteen city capital budgets combined. The third and fourth ranked categories (housing and higher education) were each significantly smaller and, as noted above, are affected by problems of comparability.

City Exempt Funds • Because of the limited nature of the debt limit exemption allowed by the state construction, city funds from this source have also been highly concentrated, as illustrated in table 5:

• The water pollution control exemption accounted for 57 percent of all exempt appropriations, primarily for treatment plant construction.

- The water supply exemption accounted for another 25 percent, about equally divided between the supply system (including the Third City Water Tunnel) and the distribution feeder systems.

- All other exempt categories accounted for the remaining 20 percent, with most of it represented by revenue-producing parking facilities and economic development projects (markets, piers, etc.).

Prior to the fiscal crisis, the major constraint on the use of funds exempt from the constitutional debt limit was the ultimate economic cost to the real estate taxpayer. This was not, however, a very binding constraint in a city whose residents are dominantly renters, where no referenda are required to approve bond issues, and where the tax cost is imposed years after the appropriation. Since the fiscal crisis, exempt funds have represented a drain on scarce bond-selling capacity equivalent to that of capital funds within the limit; this has markedly influenced city budgeting practices with regard to them.

Table 5

CITY EXEMPT FUNDS, SELECTED CATEGORIES,
FISCAL YEARS 1966–79

Category	Amount ($ millions)	Percent of Total
Water Pollution Control:		
Plants	746.0	37.6
Sewers	381.3	19.2
Sub-total, Pollution Control	1,127.3	56.8
Water Supply and Distribution:		
Supply Facilities	212.2	10.7
Mains	252.7	12.7
Sub-total, Water	464.9	23.4
Economic Development	277.7	14.0
Traffic Facilities	43.3	2.2
All Other Categories	70.7	3.6
TOTAL	1,983.9	100.0

SOURCE: New York City Capital Budgets, 1966–79.

City Debt Limit Funds • The residual source of funds for the city's capital program is bond funds within the constitutional limit. These have accounted for just over half (54 percent) of all capital budget appropriations since 1966.

Debt limit appropriations have been less heavily concentrated by function than have intergovernmental aid or exempt funds. The two largest functional categories in the 1966–79 period were elementary and secondary education (22.5 percent of thirteen-year total debt limit appropriations) and transit (13.9 percent). Together, these two categories accounted for just over one-third of all debt limit appropriations. No other category achieved comparable weighting.

Capital
Program
Expenditures

Capital budget appropriations are usually (but not always) translated into expenditures, either in the fiscal year of their appropriation or subsequently. During most of the period 1966–79 city charter provisions allowed capital appropriations, once enacted, to remain valid until either expended or rescinded because they were no longer needed or appropriate.

Some of the items in the city's capital budget lend themselves to rapid translation into expenditures. This was especially true of the operating costs included in prior budgets. Other items take years or even decades to move from appropriation to expenditure, despite the city's stated objective of appropriating only those funds it anticipates expending in the year covered by each capital budget. Delays in design contract award, approvals, bidding, and at a host of other points in the cycle of design and construction afflict not only New York City but every major municipality's construction program. In extreme cases, items can become involved in interminable litigation: the acquisition of a park site at Breezy Point is one such case where for nearly ten years the appropriation could be neither spent nor rescinded.

Additional factors that obstruct comparison of construction award data with capital budget appropriation data are:

- In at least two categories (higher education and health and hospitals) available construction award data includes contracts issued by state agencies that produced buildings for the city. Generally, these projects were financed under contractual agreements and never appeared as capital budget appropriations.

- Many of the items in the capital budget are not infrastructure elements, or even structural components at all. For example, land and equipment purchases account for significant fractions of the budget.

29

Beyond the factors already cited, it should be noted that even data on actual construction awards is subject to some of the time lags noted above: it may take two or more years to complete complex construction projects even after the contract has been awarded.

THE CITY'S CONSTRUCTION PROGRAM

Overall trends in the city's construction program are shown in figure 3. There was a continuing rise in city construction awards beginning in 1969 and continuing until 1973, with the exception of the single year 1971. The increase was in substantial measure the direct result of policy decisions by the Lindsay administration in 1966 to revitalize the city's construction program which had become stagnant in the later period of the Wagner administration. The time necessary to initiate design so that new projects could begin construction are responsible for the continuing low level of awards in fiscal years 1966 to 1968. The sharp drop in construction award levels in fiscal 1971 also had its origins in a policy decision: in an effort to induce construction contractors and unions to increase the level of minority employment in the city's capital program, Mayor Lindsay imposed a moratorium on all projects that failed to meet the city's equal opportunity targets; the issue was compromised after fiscal 1971 and it appears likely that part of the awards in the peak years of 1972 and 1973 actually represent projects ready to go in 1971 but held up by the moratorium.

City construction awards declined in the years following 1973 with the steepest drop following the onset of the fiscal crisis. The only construction programs that continued at relatively high levels in fiscal years 1975 to 1978 were for transit and water pollution control treatment plants, categories for which substantial amounts of federal and state aid was available. In fiscal 1975, the transit program alone accounted for 71 percent of all city construction awards (in contrast to its longer-term share of about 16 percent).

MAJOR CONSTRUCTION PRIORITIES

New York City's construction program went into high gear in the years following 1968 as a result of deliberate efforts by the Lindsay administration to speed the planning and construction of capital facilities to fulfill major municipal needs and also to take advantage

FIGURE 3.

CONSTRUCTION AWARDS BY NEW YORK CITY AGENCIES, FISCAL YEARS 1966-1978.

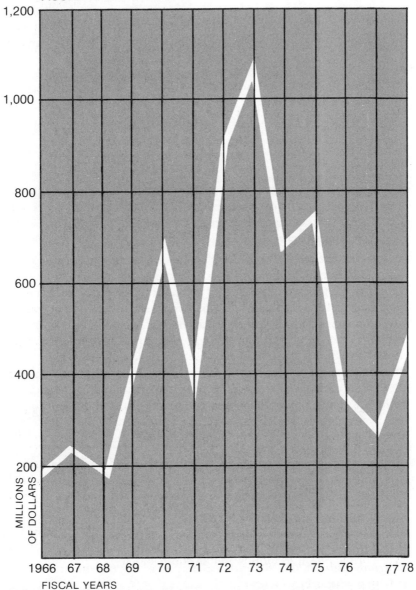

of available borrowing capacity. The pace of construction starts rose rapidly from 1968 to 1973 (except during the 1971 self-imposed "moratorium"). The chief components of this surge of capital construction were schools and water pollution control facilities, although three other programs were also of great importance: higher education, water supply, and transit. Some indication of the factors underlying trends in these priority areas are presented below.

Elementary and Secondary Education • Total enrollment in city schools peaked in about 1971 at 1,137,500 students and has been falling since then; it is expected to drop to less than a million pupils by 1980. However, the leveling off and decline of school enrollments still left the city with needs on which there was widespread agreement, such as:

- Large population shifts within the city left close-in ghetto areas seriously overcrowded even as enrollment declines emptied schools in outlying parts of the city. These changes left severe capacity problems even after an extensive free-choice busing program.

- As the "baby boom" moved through the school system, the need for increased capacity continued to grow in the high schools (at least until 1975) even though elementary enrollment peaked as early as 1970.

- Many of the city's existing schools had been built in the 1920s or earlier and were seriously obsolete and worn out. In addition, changes to introduce such concepts as a 4-4-4 grade system and "comprehensive" high schools created a need for new facilities by virtue of educational policy change.

Schools have long had the most effective political lobby for new construction in New York City. Its political effectiveness survived almost intact despite wrangles over integration and declining enrollments. It was not until the fiscal crisis cut back sharply on school construction that central budget and planning staffs were given a real opportunity to try to eliminate the least-needed of the "political" school projects. Even now, it remains to be seen if the restoration of construction capacity in the post–1978 period will not also see a revival of the pressures for new school construction.

Water Pollution Control • A combination of carrot-and-stick behavior at the state and federal levels lies behind the city's surge in the construction of water pollution control treatment facilities.

The "carrot" was in the form of aid provided by the state and federal governments to reduce the city share of new plant construction and upgrading of existing plants to only about 10 percent of total cost. The "stick" was regulation by the same governments mandating sharply increased standards of water condition. To meet these standards, the city has undertaken construction of three giant new plants (Newtown Creek, North River, and Red Hook) and very costly reconstruction or upgrading of its other existing plants.

Two of the three new giant plants still have major components to be completed: the superstructure of the North River plant and the whole new plant at Red Hook in Brooklyn. It is anticipated that most of the cost of these facilities will be financed by intergovernmental grants, although at one point the Nixon administration impounded some three-quarters of a billion dollars in federal grants for the city's water pollution control program. Subsequently, the situation improved—in large part as a result of successful court action the city took to oppose the federal impoundments.

Higher Education • Policy decisions to maintain free tuition and introduce "open enrollment" at City University in the late 1960s resulted in a massive surge in enrollments in the 1970s. The increased student body was housed in a scattered array of leased facilities (supermarkets, offices, apartments, old schools, etc.) while the university planned a system of twenty new or expanded campuses. Peak enrollment of 187,000 students was reached in 1975, at a time when the new campus construction effort was barely getting into full gear. The fiscal crisis caused four major projects (costing $300 million) to be frozen in mid-construction; most are still in that uncomfortable status. City University enrollment is now down at least 15 percent from its 1975 peak and is continuing to drop, partly because the fiscal crisis brought an end to the policy of open enrollment and free tuition, and partly because a general decline in college applications has set in across the nation. Currently, a mayoral committee is reviewing the university's cut-down master construction plan to see if even the reduced-size version is acceptable.

Water Supply • There was only one major project that affected trends in this category: the Third City Tunnel. The complex misadventures that beset this project have left the city with an unusable $200 million facility that may cost $600 million to complete (for the first stage alone, not to speak of the remaining four stages). This project is discussed in some detail in part II of this study.

Transit • The city and the state of New York made a billion-dollar commitment to a "Grand Design" for expanding the transit system in the late 1960's. The centerpiece of the expansion was to be a new Second Avenue subway from the Battery to Co-op City in the North Bronx, plus other new lines in Queens and Brooklyn.

The slow pace of design meant that relatively little new transit construction got under way before the crisis of 1975. However, the introduction of massive amounts of federal aid for transit made this program substantially "freeze-proof." Thus, transit construction resisted the sharp drop that beset all other city construction programs in 1976.

One additional factor kept transit construction going in the post-crisis years: the city "borrowed" federal construction grants and used them for operating subsidies to the transit fare under a provision of federal law* generally attributed to former Mayor Abraham D. Beame. The "Beame shuffle," as it became known in New York, gave fare relief at the expense of an unbreakable commitment to invest equivalent amounts of city and state funds for transit construction in transit. Thus, in fiscal 1976 , transit construction alone accounted for $224 million or 71 percent of the total city construction awards of $316 million.

CONSTRUCTION AWARDS BY FUNCTIONAL CATEGORIES

Table 6 presents summary data on actual construction awards by major functional categories for the fiscal 1966 to 1978 period. Year by year data for the same categories are presented in table 7.

Over half of all construction awards in the twelve-year period described in the tables were concentrated in three categories: school construction, sewage treatment, and transit. In approximately equal shares, these were the major priorities of New York's construction program.

SELECTED FUNCTIONAL TRENDS

Construction trends for each of the last twelve years are shown in figure 4 for the selected infrastructure categories which are of par-

---

* Section 3(h) of the Surface Transportation Act of 1978. Under this provision, a locality could borrow up to one-half of its federal transit capital grant and use it for operating purposes provided that it then repaid the capital funds from local sources (in New York City's case, from state or city capital funds).

Table 6

CONSTRUCTION AWARDS BY MAJOR FUNCTIONAL CATEGORIES, FISCAL YEARS 1966 TO 1978

Category	Amount of Awards ($ millions)	Percent of Total
Economic Development (Ports and Terminals)	135	2.0
Elementary and Secondary Education	1,326	19.6
Higher Education	543	8.0
Water Pollution Control:		
Treatment Plants	1,186	17.4
Sewers	343	5.1
Water Supply and Distribution	374	5.5
Sanitation	60	0.9
Health and Hospitals	513	7.6
General Services (Public Buildings)	565	8.3
Parks and Museums	228	3.4
Highways	316	4.7
Traffic	45	0.6
Transit	1,145	16.9
TOTAL	6,779	100.0

SOURCE: Office of the Director of Construction and Office of Management and Budget, 1966–78.

ticular concern in this study. The figure suggests that there has been considerable variability from one year to the next, a common characteristic of capital construction activity. Among the extreme variations, the most notable are:

- Award of the construction contract for the first stage of the Third City Water Tunnel (a major link between the reservoirs and the distribution system) was made in 1970.

- Massive awards for construction and upgrading of components of the water pollution control treatment plan system occurred in 1972 and 1973.

- Major awards on components of the Transit Authority's "Grand Design" for extension of its track and tunnels were made in 1975 and 1976.

The effect of the fiscal crisis is also visible in this chart, reflected in the "bottoming-out" of all programs except transit in 1976. Transit continued at a high level primarily because of federal aid commitments.

Table 7
CONSTRUCTION AWARDS BY FUNCTIONAL CATEGORIES, FISCAL YEARS 1966–78
(in $ millions)

Function or Agency	1966	1967	1968	1969	1970	1971	1972	1973	1974	1975	1976	1977	1978
Economic Development	—	—	—	—	—	—	—	28	44	35	16	5	17
Board of Education[a]	85	73	35	175	135	112	211	191	148	103	5	27	27
Higher Education[b]	12	19	33	39	54	11	11	1	99	217	9	11	28
Water Pollution Control:													
Plants	17	4	29	15	79	34	297	477	63	20	30	12	110
Sewers	8	10	8	16	24	49	28	61	30	37	7	24	41
Water Supply and Distribution	4	15	3	4	223	4	14	21	12	16	12	40	6
Sanitation	—	—	—	—	—	—	—	1	15	5	—	6	32
Health and Hospitals[c]	36	47	4	14	31	58	26	54	17	12	2	7	12
General Services	12	26	24	122	13	35	70	116	78	30	5	15	20
Parks and Museums	9	10	24	24	27	17	22	24	23	24	4	5	15
Highways	12	15	21	23	22	22	19	36	31	19	2	30	'65
Traffic	—	—	1	4	3	3	—	13	13	10	—	—	—
Transit	11	30	36	28	113	62	28	89	135	236	224	75	79
TOTALS	204	248	216	464	723	407	920	1112	698	762	316	257	452

NOTES: [a] Board of Education includes Educational Construction Fund.
[b] Higher Education includes City University Construction Fund.
[c] Health and Hospitals includes State Facilities Corporation.

SOURCE: Office of the Director of Construction and Office of Management and Budget, New York City.

FIGURE 4.
CONSTRUCTION AWARDS IN SELECTED INFRASTRUCTURE
CATEGORIES BY NEW YORK CITY AGENCIES,
FISCAL YEARS 1966-1978.

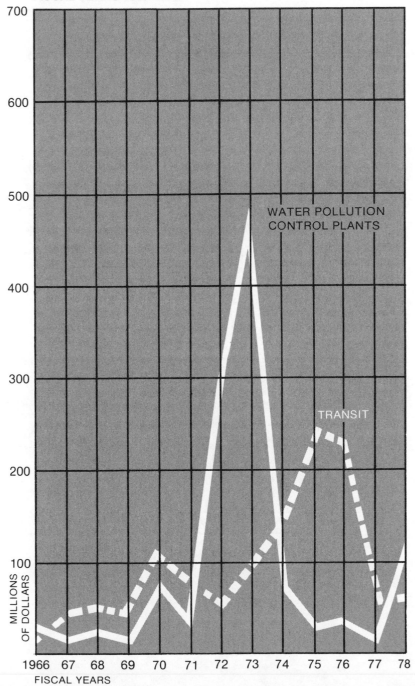

FIGURE 4.
CONSTRUCTION AWARDS IN SELECTED INFRASTRUCTURE
CATEGORIES BY NEW YORK CITY AGENCIES,
FISCAL YEARS 1966-1978.

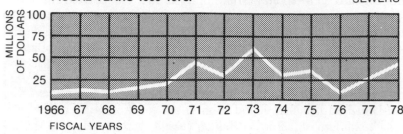

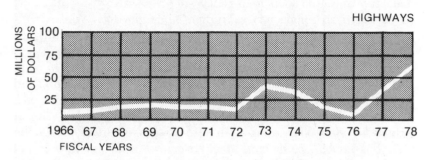

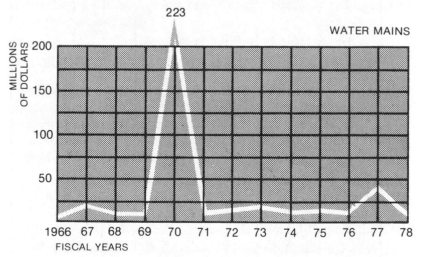

Infrastructure Maintenance Expenditures

Operation and maintenance of New York City's infrastructure system are financed through the city's expense budget. The only significant exception to this pattern was in fiscal years 1973 to 1975 when capital budget funds were appropriated for "comprehensive repair" programs and made available for school buildings, water distribution, highway, and other repair programs. This practice ended with the onset of the fiscal crisis.

EXPENSE BUDGET PRACTICES

Unfortunately, the city's expense budget is not so organized as to allow data on maintenance of the infrastructure—or even the entire capital plant—to be extracted readily. The expense budget is organized under the following hierarchy of categories:

- *Agency or department.* After adoption of the budget, funds may not be transferred between agencies except with approval of the board of estimate and the city council.

- *Unit of Appropriation.* Each agency has from two to eight units of appropriation (e.g., executive management, support functions, and operations). These units tend to have a general relationship to the agency's organizational structure, but only rarely are maintenance functions of sufficient size to be grouped together in a separate unit of appropriation. Funds can be transferred among units of appropriation within an agency with the approval of the mayor. An exception to this practice exists in the Transit Authority whose operating budget is wholly separate from that of the city. The TA budget does list maintenance activities separately.

- *Responsibility Centers.* In recent years many city agencies grouped activities within units of appropriation by "responsibility centers" which are related activities under jurisdiction of a single manager. Unfortunately, comparable data are not generally available over any significant period of time; in addition, few agencies have defined maintenance functions as responsibility centers.

- *Budget Lines.* At the lowest level of detail, the entire expense budget consists of hundreds of thousands of individual "lines." A line may describe one job (position name and salary) or a group of identical jobs or it may characterize a unit of OTPS (Other Than Personal Services), such as supplies, rent, and travel. Because of the large number of lines, plus the fact that many describe unfilled positions, it is not feasible to assemble lines into meaningful functional units unless an agency has done so for its own analytic or control purposes.

For these reasons, it did not prove feasible in this study to obtain consistent information on maintenance activities comparable to the capital budget and construction award data presented previously. Instead, attention was focused on four infrastructure components (water, sewers, highways, and transit) and the data-gathering effort was directed toward obtaining specific information from each of the agencies involved.

TRANSIT MAINTENANCE

Reflecting the great importance that physical plant has for the operations of the Transit Authority, that agency organizes its budget into categories that are specifically focused on maintenance. There are three such categories (or "budgets" in Transit Authority parlance):

- Maintenance of the rapid transit right-of-way, consisting of the tracks, tunnels, elevated structures, stations, electrical substations, signals, and other fixed physical components of the system.

- Maintenance of the more than 6,000 subway cars.
- Maintenance of the Authority's buses.

Data on the staffing levels available and on funds budgeted for each of these three functions in fiscal years 1970 through 1979 are presented in tables 8 and 9.

The size of the maintenance staff peaked in fiscal year 1971 at just under 15,000 workers. The number remained above 14,000 until 1977 when fiscal pressures caused it to drop below 13,000. By fiscal year 1979 the number of maintenance workers was 17 percent below the peak level of 1971.

Each of the three subcategories followed a different pattern. The number of employees on the right-of-way maintenance staff held relatively steady throughout the period 1970–79. Subway car maintenance staff was reduced significantly and by 1979 was 32 percent below the peak reached in 1971. Bus maintenance staff tended to increase throughout the period, peaking in 1976 but remaining close to that level through fiscal 1979.

Expenditures followed rather different patterns than did staffing,

Table 8

TRANSIT AUTHORITY PERSONNEL INVOLVED IN MAINTENANCE ACTIVITIES
(Full-Time Employees)

Fiscal Year	Rapid Transit Maintenance of Way	Car Maintenance	Surface Maintenance	Total Maintenance Staff
1979	6,062	4,524	1,921	12,507
1978[a]	N/A	N/A	N/A	N/A
1977	6,133	4,975	1,888	12,996
1976	6,803	5,520	2,040	14,363
1975	6,826	5,622	1,951	14,399
1974	6,806	5,889	1,738	14,433
1973	6,659	5,861	1,634	14,154
1972	6,680	6,412	1,626	14,718
1971	6,704	6,698	1,695	15,097
1970	6,300	5,232	1,672	13,204

[a] The Transit Authority did not adopt a comprehensive budget fiscal year 1978.
SOURCE: New York City, Transit Authority Budgets, 1970–79.

Table 9
MAINTENANCE EXPENDITURES FOR SELECTED FUNCTIONS,
NEW YORK CITY TRANSIT AUTHORITY, FISCAL YEARS 1970–79
(in $ millions)

Fiscal Year	Rapid Transit Maintenance of Highway			Car Maintenance			Bus Maintenance		
	Salaries	Materials	Other	Salaries	Materials	Other	Salaries	Materials	Other
1979	110.5	20.3	8.8*	79.7	16.3	4.4	34.2	16.2	3.2
1978	105.7	16.8	2.1	78.1	17.3	5.1	33.0	14.7	2.2
1977	99.8	15.4	2.8	84.3	21.1	5.7	30.8	15.0	2.0
1976	108.8	14.2	2.5	95.8	24.4	7.7	34.8	13.7	2.0
1975	94.4	10.9	2.2	82.8	21.0	7.0	29.1	11.5	1.8
1974	89.0	9.4	4.1	83.6	20.0	6.5	25.1	6.8	1.4
1973	81.7	8.2	3.0	79.0	19.6	5.9	22.3	6.2	1.3
1972	76.2	7.9	3.5	74.0	13.2	6.1	20.0	5.7	1.3
1971	68.3	7.2	2.3	67.8	11.4	4.5	18.8	5.5	1.2
1970	59.6	6.7	1.8	49.0	8.9	3.3	17.0	5.1	1.0

* Data not comparable to earlier years because of a change in budgetary practice.
SOURCE: New York City, Transit Authority Budgets, 1970–79.

mainly because of the increasing costs of salaries and materials. The effects of the city's fiscal crisis are reflected in the transit maintenance budgets in 1977 when each of the three categories suffered a dollar reduction (and an even greater reduction if inflation were to be taken into account). By 1979, the dollar levels budgeted in 1976 had been reached once again, but by now with significantly less purchasing power as indicated by the drop in the number of full-time staff available for maintenance of the system.

The sharp cutbacks in subway car maintenance were somewhat compensated for by the delivery of substantial numbers of new cars to the Transit Authority during the 1970–1979 period, and by reduced service on many lines. In addition, this was an area where productivity gains could be made through utilization of more modern maintenance equipment and machinery. Even with these compensating features, however, the casual observer can readily see how neglected maintenance has affected the city's subway fleet.

OTHER SELECTED AREAS

Data on trends in maintenance staffing and maintenance expenditures are much less readily available with respect to highways, water distribution, and sewers than is the case for transit. The following information is presented as a general indication of trends in these areas.

Highways and Bridges • Table 10 presents data on some indicators of maintenance staffing in the city's Department of Transportation. From fiscal 1976 to 1978, a period when general city staffing was cut by about 20 percent under the impact of the fiscal crisis, these maintenance functions, taken collectively, managed to hold level (after a drop of about 9 percent from fiscal 1976 to 1977). The overall pattern, however, included a significant increase (85 percent) in the arterial highway repair program—where Highway Department responsibilities were expanded to include functions formerly performed by the Parks Department—and declines in the other categories of street maintenance, bridge and structure repair, and inspection. The federal Comprehensive Employment Training Act program helped keep job losses below what might have otherwise occurred.

Data on the man-days of work devoted to maintenance activities on the city's bridges and other highway structures during the

Table 10

STAFFING OF HIGHWAY AND BRIDGE MAINTENANCE AND REPAIR FUNCTIONS, NEW YORK CITY DEPARTMENT OF TRANSPORTATION

Maintenance Staffing (Full-Time Employees)

Function	Fiscal Years		
	1976	1977	1978
Street maintenance	1,158	944	911
Bridge and structure repair	413	391	393
Arterial highway repair	160	136	297
Inspection and investigation	103	83	91
Total	1,834	1,672	1,835

Repair of Bridges and Structures (Man-days)

Function	Fiscal Years				
	1974	1975	1976	1977	1978
Painting	5,247	4,817	4,325	3,995[a]	3,956
Steel Work	8,892	10,351	9,024	8,824[a]	10,300

[a] Plan data, not actual.

SOURCE: Management Plan Reports (1974 to 1978), New York City Department of Transportation.

1974–78 period indicate a continuing decline in manpower available for painting (a preventive activity) while the manpower devoted to the more evident need to make steel work repairs held roughly constant over the five years.

Sewers • Over the ten year period 1968–78, the number of workers available for sewer maintenance declined by 35 percent from 692 to 514. Despite this sharp cutback, the deputy director of the Sewer Division in the city's Department of Environmental Protection believes that the level of maintenance work has been kept at a nearly constant level.* The reasons for this gain in productivity are (a) an

---

* Based on statements during interview.

expansion of the number of catch basin cleaning machines, including the introduction of a machine especially adapted to New York City conditions, and (b) the introduction of TV equipment to examine sewers rapidly and efficiently. TV inspection has been done under contract with private firms.

Water • The number of full-time employees available to the Water Division of the Department of Environmental Protection (formerly the Department of Water Resources) dropped by 28 percent (from 664 to 479) over the period 1970 to 1977. During this period at least one major component of the agency's workload—the repair of water-line breaks—remained roughly constant, as will be detailed in part II. Total repairs, of leaks as well as breaks, rose by 28 percent from 1970 to 1977 in direct contrast to the decline in available manpower.

THE NEED FOR BETTER DATA

In the past year and a half, New York City agencies have begun more comprehensive planning to address the needs of the city's infrastructure. Part III of this report details the planning that formed the basis for the city's request to Congress for long-term loan guarantees. However, research done for this report indicates that the present approach to examining needs and programming capital investment in the infrastructure has not yet been extended to maintenance and repair functions. Neither the city's central planning agencies (the Office of Management and Budget and the Department of City Planning) nor the operating agencies have yet focused on this issue in anything like a systematic fashion. There is an absence of both data with which to assess the adequacy of maintenance activity and of any coordinated plan or planning process. The city's management plan, an impressive and extensive body of measures of performance in the delivery of city services, generally lacks any consistent measures of maintenance (except for isolated critical problems, such as out-of-service measures for sanitation collection trucks).

Given the proposed emphasis on infrastructure investment in the next decade, it would seem appropriate for the city to devote specific sections of the management plan to infrastructure maintenance reporting. In addition, the city should undertake detailed examination—probably on the basis of statistical sampling—to ascer-

tain the effects of prior maintenance on the condition of critical infrastructure components. Without such direct analysis of the infrastructure (going well beyond what has been possible within the scope
of this study) New York City's decision makers will not be in a position to make valid choices on the importance of maintenance functions vis-à-vis other pressing demands on the city's operating budget.

Part 2
Physical Condition of the Infrastructure

Authority for Development and Maintenance

One useful way to examine New York City's approach to the development and maintenance of its physical infrastructure is to look at it in terms of three mission-oriented systems, each of which includes a variety of elements. The three are the public utility system, the transportation system, and the public facility system.*

THE PUBLIC UTILITY SYSTEM

The municipal components of the public utility system in New York (as contrasted with electricity, gas, and telephone services, which are provided by regulated private utilities) are described below as they existed in 1978, after a decade of numerous changes (such as unifying the Sanitation and Water Resources Departments under a single Environmental Protection Administration). The principal municipal elements of this public utility system include:

Water Supply and Distribution • The City of New York through the Department of Environmental Protection, now has virtually complete responsibility for water supply and distribution within the city. There is still one sizable private water company serving part of the Jamaica area in Queens but it seems likely that this private system will also come under public control in the next decade.

---

* The concept of this triple system is based on an approach first presented in *Capital Construction Needs of New York City in the 1977–1986 Period* by David A. Grossman, The Twentieth Century Fund, February, 1977 (mimeo).

Most of New York's water comes from surface reservoirs in the extensive city-owned Catskill Mountains watershed and the Croton reservoir system in Westchester County. Until 1978, the major supply facilities and the aqueducts leading from them to the city were constructed under the direction of the quasi-independent Board of Water Supply whose members were appointed for life terms by the mayor. As a result of problems connected with the construction of the Third City Water Tunnel, along with other factors, the governor and legislature approved a mayoral request to integrate this board with the Department of Environmental Protection as an agency under direct mayoral control.

Waste Water Collection and Treatment • The Department of Environmental Protection also has responsibility for the construction, maintenance, and operation of the city's sanitary and storm sewer system and for the pollution control plants that treat waste water before discharging it into the major bodies of water that border the city.

Solid Waste Collection and Disposal • New York City's Department of Sanitation is responsible for collecting solid wastes from residential structures; commercial and industrial establishments must, by city regulation, arrange for private collection. The Department of Sanitation also operates a system of incinerators and sanitary landfills for disposing of all solid wastes, whether residential or other.

THE TRANSPORTATION SYSTEM

New York City is the focus of one of the world's most complex transportation systems, whose sea, land, and air components are under the jurisdiction of a broad variety of public and private organizations. The principal elements of this system include:

Streets and Highways • The New York City Department of Transportation has jurisdiction over most of the more than 6,000 miles of paved streets and highways within the city. Its bridge division is responsible for the large East River bridges and the many other bridges and structures. The department also coordinates development of the arterial highway network within the city. Major system elements are, however, constructed or financed by other agencies: the State Department of Transportation has principal responsibility for the interstate expressway system; the Triborough Bridge and Tunnel Authority (now part of the region-serving Metropolitan Transportation Authority) built and operates a series of major bridges and tunnels; and the Port Authority of New York and New Jersey built and operates cross-Hudson vehicular bridges and tunnels.

Mass Transit • The New York City Transit Authority, another unit of the Metropolitan Transit Authority, constructs and operates the rapid transit system in the four most populous boroughs and, through a subsidiary, on Staten Island as well. While management of the transit system is under MTA jurisdiction, the Transit Authority's capital program is part of the city's capital budget, and title to all facilities (whether financed by city, state or federal funds) is vested in the city. A cross-Hudson rapid transit system (PATH) is owned and operated by the Port Authority. Public bus service is provided by the Transit Authority both directly and through an operating subsidiary. In addition, there are many private bus companies that provide both local and express services.

Commuter and Freight Rail • The extensive commuter rail service of the New York region is under jurisdiction of the MTA which also, through its Long Island Rail Road unit, provides part of the region's freight service. The remainder of the freight service is mostly under the jurisdiction of Conrail, a federally-initiated conglomerate that has assumed responsibility for Penn Central operations. AMTRAK, a federal corporation, operates intercity long-distance passenger rail service.

Airports • The region's three major airports are Port Authority facilities. LaGuardia and Kennedy are located within New York City; the third is Newark Airport in New Jersey. The city owns a small airport in Flushing, Queens, that it leases to a private operator.

Ports and Terminals • New York City's Department of Ports and Terminals owns and operates a variety of major terminal facilities including wholesale food markets as well as docks and piers. The Port Authority, either directly or by arrangement with the city, operates container-handling facilities and the new passenger ship terminal. The city's Department of Traffic constructs and operates parking garages and open parking areas to serve commuters and business centers.

Ferries • The Department of Transportation operates the Staten-Island-to-Manhattan ferry system.

THE PUBLIC FACILITIES SYSTEM

In addition to the capital networks described above, there are many public facilities which are involved in the delivery of public services. The most capital-intensive of these facilities are described below.

Education • The city's 900 public school buildings and the Fashion Institute of Technology (a two-year college) are constructed and operated by the city Board of Education. In recent years some combined-use facilities containing schools as well as commercial or residential facilities were built by the Educational Construction Fund, a public corporation. The twenty colleges of City University are under the jurisdiction of the Board of Higher Education; their construction programs, however, are operated through the City University Construction Fund and are actually implemented by the New York State Dormitory Authority, both of which are state-chartered public corporations.

Health and Hospitals • The Health and Hospitals Corporation is a quasi-independent city agency which operates the city's extensive public hospital system. In recent years a number of hospitals and other health facilities were financed and built by state agencies under contract to the city.

Parks and Museums • The Department of Parks has responsibility for constructing and operating the city's large and wide-spread park, playground, and recreation facility system. The city also finances a substantial part of the cultural institution system, owning such facilities as the Metropolitan Museum, the New York Public Library, and the Museum of Natural History. These facilities are supervised by the city's Department of Cultural Affairs, with capital program assistance from the city's Department of General Services. Two recent developments have introduced state and federal park agencies into the city: the state's Department of Natural Resources has begun to develop facilities within the city; and the National Park Service has taken over responsibility for Gateway National Park, which stretches from Fire Island to the New Jersey shore with extensive components within the city limits.

Other Public Buildings • The city's Department of General Services constructs (and in some cases, operates) buildings for city agencies such as the correction, police, and fire departments, the three systems of branch libraries, and the courts. It is also responsible for the construction and maintenance of most city-owned office buildings.

Industrial Parks • New York City provides industrial park facilities at a number of locations, such as the former Brooklyn Navy Yard, Flatlands Industrial Park in Brooklyn, and College Point Industrial Park in Queens. A small but growing fraction of the city's industrial jobs are located in such centers.

COMPLEXITY IN FINANCE AND ADMINISTRATION

The pattern described above involves a complex combination of responsibilities for the development of the physical infrastructure; in some cases, different agencies are responsible for construction and maintenance of the same facility. Also, the pattern has often changed over the past decade—at times in ways that bewilder even close observers—as responsibilities for capital finance and administration have shifted between the city and the state and within these levels of government.

During Lindsay's terms as mayor (1966–73), a major restructuring occurred with the integration of numerous small mayoral agencies into a group of functionally-oriented "administrations." Under these administrations responsibilities were grouped along functional lines (environmental protection, human services, health services, etc.), rather than by organizational structure; hence one form of integration often meant fractionalization elsewhere. For example, the Public Works Department of the Wagner era lost its bridge-building function to the Lindsay-era Transportation Administration; its responsibility for sewers and the building of sewage treatment plants to the Environmental Protection Administration; and its responsibility for the construction and rehabilitation of hospitals to the Health and Hospitals Corporation. What was left in the Department of Public Works was much less than what was removed to the other agencies, and the department itself became a component of the Municipal Services Administration.

During the succeeding four years under Mayor Beame, a number of additional changes were made, mostly consisting of taking apart Mayor Lindsay's functionally organized administrations. For example, the Environmental Protection Administration was divided into two major agencies, the Departments of Environmental Protection and Sanitation; in the process, the Department of Water Resources became several divisions within Environmental Protection. Few of the construction functions were shifted in the Beame period, although the public works agency (once the independent Department of Public Works, then a department within an integrated Municipal Services Administration, then a public buildings division within a General Services Department) gained responsibility for the museums and institutions overseen by the newly independent Department of Cultural Affairs.

In its turn, the Koch Administration, which took office in 1978, is once again restructuring city agencies, although, to date, it has not involved major reorganization of the building functions.

A second trend over the last fifteen years was the multiplication of quasi-independent public benefit corporations under the state administration of Governor Nelson Rockefeller. Some were assigned bond-issuing authority, some construction authority, and some both. One reason for their creation was to avoid the state's constitutional limitations on debt issuance (which required hard-to-pass referenda) by the issuance of "moral obligation" bonds. This concept was invented for New York State by former U.S. Attorney General John Mitchell, who was then a bond counsel in private practice. Another reason for their creation was to avoid the slow bureaucratic processes of the state's public works agencies. These state corporations were imitated by similar state-authorized public benefit corporations initiated by the city. The public benefit corporations sought to expand their roles in the field of capital construction until a city agency head who wanted to undertake the design and construction of a new facility would have up to half a dozen different organizations from which to select his agent. For example, when the city's deputy mayor for criminal justice recently began investigating how to plan and construct several new detention facilities located near the criminal courts (to be financed by the sale of city prisons on Rikers Island to the state to house sentenced prisoners) he could choose one of the following five organizations to undertake the task:

- The public buildings division of the General Services Department (the remnant of the once-dominant city Public Works Department).

- Three different New York State public benefit corporations: the Urban Development Corporation (whose original purpose was primarily to construct moderate income housing); the Facilities Development Corporation (originally established to build hospitals and mental health facilities) and the Dormitory Authority (originally established to construct student housing at private colleges).

- The multi-state Port Authority of New York and New Jersey.

In addition, financing arrangements were available to him through diverse resources such as the Municipal Assistance Corporation or other state agencies, through the sale of city bonds to municipal employee pension funds, or through direct appropriation by the state to one of its corporations (as in the compensation for the city prisons on Rikers Island).

There are no easy guides to this complex maze of agencies and options. In fact, the preceding description is so simplified that it omits important considerations such as the ability to award on the basis of competitive bidding vs. negotiated contracts, as well as the choice between civil service engineers and private consultants for the design and supervision of construction.

TRACKING CITY CONSTRUCTION

The broad array of possibilities available to carry out aspects of the city's construction program raises significant problems not only for the analyst who wants to measure what has happened but also for the mayor and his Office of Management and Budget who want to track progress and control expenditures.

Two major steps taken in the Lindsay administration provided some overall measures of monitoring and control. First, the city's Budget Bureau (now the Office of Management and Budget) worked with individual city agencies to construct critical-path, network-based, management-information systems for each major construction program. Built to reasonably standardized specifications, these agency-based systems were unified through common use of the Budget Bureau's computer and a common "logic" in system design. Second, the mayor and comptroller concurred in the establishment of a central Board of Construction (consisting of a director of construction, the budget director, and the first deputy comptroller). This board, relying largely on the computerized management information system, was able to identify and address specific blockages and breakdowns in design and construction as they occurred.

Unfortunately, the city's fiscal crisis, which brought construction to a near halt by 1976, was paralleled by serious deterioration in both the capital-construction management information system and the capacity and staffing of the Board of Construction. As the prospects for an expanded city construction program appear (see part III, below) it has become necessary for the city to restore these two critical operations to something like their former effectiveness. Success in this regard, or the development of viable alternatives, is likely to be a strong determinant of the city's ability to mount a large-scale construction effort.

CHANGES IN CAPITAL BUDGETING AND PROGRAMMING

Revisions in the city charter proposed by a state commission and adopted by the city's voters in 1975 made substantial changes in capital budget procedures which had been in existence since a completely new charter was adopted in 1965. Some of the changes follow:

- The City Planning Commission's role in preparing the initial draft of the capital budget and a five year capital program was eliminated. The commission now is limited to preparing a needs and priorities analysis which is intended to guide budget and program preparation.

- The Office of Management and Budget (OMB) now prepares the draft and executive capital budgets as well as the three-year capital program. Under the new charter provisions, the program as well as the budget must be adopted by the Board of Estimate and the City Council, unlike the earlier five-year program which had no direct effect on either of these two bodies.

- OMB's control over the details of the capital program was constrained by establishment of mandatory limits on the type and timing of its review. At the same time, additional review powers over specific projects (as to site and design) were extended to the city's 59 locally-based Community Boards as well as the Board of Estimate. It is still too soon to see what effect these changes will have on either slowing or speeding capital construction.

The 1975 charter amendments made no direct changes in capital program finance procedures except to mandate the phasing-out of any use of the capital budget to finance operating expenditures. Mayor Koch has committed the city to achieve this goal within a five-year period, rather than the ten years allowed in the charter.

Another change that was made a decade earlier in the city charter is also worthy of mention because of its significant effects on infrastructure development. Before 1965, the cost of installing water and sewer lines and streets was charged partly to the abutting property owners. These charges were often substantial, especially in the developing single-family residential areas of Queens and Staten Island. A major factor in obtaining approval of the 1965 charter (which also shifted the responsibility for constructing sewers and streets from the five borough presidents to the mayor) was acceptance of the cost of all such improvements as city capital projects. As might readily be imagined, the change had dramatic effects on the attitudes of property owners toward infrastructure investment in water lines, sewers, and streets. Demand soared, and neighborhoods that had resisted the imposition of requirements for adequate infrastructure suddenly became their most vocal advocates.

The Infrastructure Inventory

INTRODUCTION

New York City does not possess anything that remotely re-
sembles a comprehensive and consistent inventory of its municipal
physical plant. It is just beginning to move toward the development
of such an inventory, largely as a by-product of the stricter accounting
standards imposed on it by the federal and state monitors of its
finances. One of these requirements is for the city to have an annual
audit of its finances by an independent outside accountant. The first
such audit covers fiscal year 1978, and one of the exceptions taken
by the auditors (Peat, Marwick, and Mitchell) was that the city
had no inventory or accounting system for its fixed assets. In response,
the City Comptroller has retained another accounting firm (Ernst
and Ernst) to design a fixed asset accounting system.

Discussions of the nature and coverage of that system have only
begun as of this writing, so little can be said about it. In fact, one
of the still unresolved issues is whether or not the system should
extend to the four infrastructure components on which this study is
focused: water, sewers, streets, and transit facilities. It seems clear,
however, that the initial focus will be on the city's stock of public
buildings and land and that the major infrastructure components will
be added only at a later date, if at all.

Another indicator of the undeveloped state of city infrastructure
records is that there is no standard-base map which can be used to
locate streets and underground utilities. Each city agency uses its
own maps and they vary considerably in scale and quality. Private
utilities also have their own maps, which display some of the same
shortcomings as those of city agencies. This lack of a standard-base
map is a serious problem in a city whose underground facilities are
as extensive and complex as any in the world. Buried in the bed of a

single New York City street can be high pressure water mains up to six feet in diameter, storm and sanitary sewers, electric, telephone, and telegraph conduits, fire alarm signal lines, steam pipes, and even more than one four-track subway. In one notable case, Park Avenue's upper reaches conceal the main line of the Penn Central railroad!

There has been little progress in preparing a unified-base map. To develop one is an extremely complex and costly step and the inability to decide whether a simple street line map should be its forerunner or whether that would delay the eventual achievement of a comprehensive surface and underground base map has obstructed a decision on either option. The cost of indecision is experienced every day as construction crews from a host of city agencies and private utilities try to cope with the interactive labyrinth that lies beneath many city streets.

The sections which follow are devoted to a summary description of four of the city's chief infrastructure components. This is not intended to be more than a brief sketch, since a full description of these systems would require maps and surveys going well beyond the scope of this analysis. It would, in fact, exceed the capacity of any of the involved public agencies to provide such a description at the present time.

WATER SUPPLY AND DISTRIBUTION

New York City's water system has long been recognized as a major municipal strength. After an initial period in the city's history when water was supplied first by open streams and ponds and then by shallow wells, far-sighted action by the city secured rights to extensive upstate watershed areas. The city then constructed a system of public distribution that reached into virtually every corner of the five boroughs. Descriptions of the supply and distribution systems follow.

The Supply System • This system brings fresh water to New York City from points as far as 125 miles away. As shown on the accompanying map (figure 5), the system is based on extensive watershed areas in the Catskill Mountains and a smaller area (the Croton watershed) in Westchester County. The Croton system, completed in 1842, was the first major component in the city's water system; the Catskill system began operation 75 years later in 1917.

Two great underground pipes, the Delaware and Catskill aque-

FIGURE 5.
NEW YORK CITY WATER SUPPLY

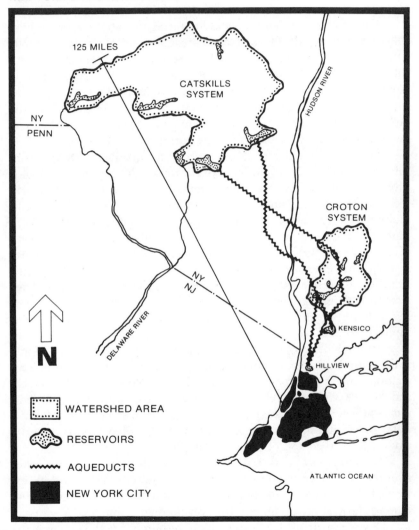

ducts, carry water from the upstate reservoir system to Kensico reservoir, located north of the city of White Plains at the southern end of the Croton watershed area. From Kensico, another aqueduct carries the water about a dozen miles south to Hillview reservoir in the Bronx. Smaller aqueducts extend directly from the Croton system into the city, bypassing Kensico and Hillview.

The reservoir system provides an average of about 1,400 million gallons per day (MGD) to New York City and about another 100 MGD to other communities in the metropolitan region. It constitutes virtually the entire fresh water supply of the city. Drawing largely from underground sources, private water companies in Queens supply a total of about 60 MGD to city residents. The city is in the process of acquiring these private companies and, within the next few years, will be responsible for the entire supply system.

The upstate watershed, reservoir, and aqueduct system constitutes an asset which would be virtually impossible to replicate today. Protection of the city's supply system, as well as its expansion to increase the dependable yield in drought years, presents difficult problems. Urban development pressures have been increasing adjacent to the Croton watershed (which accounts for about 15 percent of the total supply). Together with stricter federal standards for water quality, this encroachment may force the city to install treatment facilities sometime in the next decade. The growth of demand for recreational uses in the Catskill watershed area places a similar but less intense pressure on the quality of the remaining city water supply resources.

Another concern of the guardians of New York's water supply is the growing water demand of other counties in the metropolitan region, some of which are already supplied by New York City. Nassau and Suffolk Counties rely on ground water supplies which may not prove sufficient or be adequately protected against infiltration of salt water or pollution. Thus, regional needs are a potential threat to the city's undisturbed use of its water supplies.

To date, New York City has resisted efforts to unify its water resources into a regional or state system. The city has, however, expressed its willingness to cooperate in regional action to increase the supply, short of giving up control over its own resources.

Development of new water supply resources for the city and the surrounding region is at present focused on projects under review by the U.S. Army Corps of Engineers to obtain fresh water from the Hudson River. The use of this potential source to close an estimated 250 MGD deficit between the safe yield of the city's reservoirs and anticipated municipal need was explored in a Corps of Engineers study that proposed a $3 billion expansion of the supply and distribution systems (including an aqueduct to Long Island). This costly proposal is presently being studied by city, state, and regional agencies.

New York City's upstate reservoir and aqueduct system was originally constructed by an independent Board of Water Supply and was then operated and maintained by the city Department of Water Resources. As noted above, the Board of Water Supply and the Department of Water Resources were integrated as a new Department of Environmental Protection in 1978.

The Distribution System • The water distribution system is made up of two primary elements: the giant water tunnels that deliver water from Hillview reservoir to the city and the system of mains that connect these tunnels to individual consumers.

From Hillview reservoir, two underground tunnels extend into the city to link the watershed areas to the distribution system. City Water Tunnel 1 delivers water to the Bronx and Manhattan; City Water Tunnel 2 carries water to Queens, Brooklyn and—via the recently constructed Richmond Tunnel—to the Silver Lake storage area on Staten Island.

Tunnels 1 and 2 are now about 51 and 42 years old, respectively. Concerned with their age and the serious problems that a breakdown in either tunnel would cause, the city began construction in 1970 of the first stage of a third water tunnel. This facility, 20 to 25 feet in diameter and up to 300 feet beneath the earth's surface, was scheduled to run initially from Hillview south to mid-Manhattan and then into Queens where it would connect to Tunnel 2. Eventually, Tunnel 3 was to run in a great loop through Queens and back to Hillview and Kensico reservoirs. The first stage of construction was bid at $200 million and the assumption was that the eventual cost of the entire loop would be about $1 billion.

Unfortunately, the digging of Tunnel 3 ran into a series of delays and physical problems in its passage through deep rock beneath the city. The contractors demanded extra payments in multimillion dollar amounts and, when no agreement was reached with the city, they stopped work and launched a $200 million lawsuit to cover damage claims against the city. Because of the fiscal crisis and the city's resulting inability to foot for additional costs, work on the tunnel would have come to a halt even if the lawsuit had been compromised.

Current city estimates indicate that it would cost up to $600 million to complete the first stage of Tunnel 3. Its extension to lower

Manhattan to relieve water supply problems in that congested business district would cost another $600 million. At present, there is no source of funds to meet these costs. Until and unless such funds become available, the potential danger of breakdown in one of the two existing tunnels continues to loom as a serious threat to the city.

Apart from the great tunnels, New York City's water distribution system consists of 6,150 miles of water line ranging from 84 inches to less than 10 inches in diameter. Table 11 summarizes the characteristics of the distribution system according to type of material, location by borough, and size of pipe.

The bulk of the system (over 95 percent) is composed of cast iron pipes of various ages, strengths, and sizes. However, a significant fraction of the largest mains (over 36 inches) is composed of other materials: 43.2 percent are steel and 8.4 percent are reinforced concrete.

Of particular concern are the older cast iron pipes of less than 10 inches in diameter. The cast iron pipes laid in the earlier years of the nineteenth century were cast horizontally and, as a result, are thinner on top than on the bottom, making them more susceptible than the ductile iron pipes installed since 1970 to breakage by pressures imposed from above. In addition, current city standards call for installation of pipes at least 10 inches in diameter; however, some 3,371 miles of cast iron pipe (55 percent of the entire distribution system) fail to meet this standard.

STORM AND SANITARY SEWERS

Far less detailed inventory data are available for the city's storm, sanitary, and combined sewer systems than for the water distribution system. This is due, in large part, to historic factors in the administration of the city. Prior to the charter changes of 1965, responsibility for sewer and street construction belonged to the five borough presidents while the water system has long been primarily a centralized mayoral responsibility. Further, the city's charges for water service and the need to maintain an accurate cost base resulted in the development of a detailed statistical and accounting system for water; sewer charges, on the other hand, were traditionally based on a percentage of the water use fee.

Overall, the sewer system contains about 6,200 miles of sewers (90 percent combined), with some 90,000 catch basins and 250,000 manholes. The system varies in character by boroughs and by the

Table 11

CHARACTERISTICS OF THE WATER DISTRIBUTION SYSTEM IN NEW YORK CITY, 1976
(in thousands of lineal feet)

1. Water Distribution Lines by Type of Material and Borough

	Borough					
Material	*Manhattan*	*Bronx*	*Brooklyn*	*Queens*	*Staten Island*	*Total City*
Reinforced Concrete	4.5	1.1	24.0	70.1	45.9	145.6
Steel	70.3	155.3	253.6	345.4	35.6	860.2
Cast Iron	3,881.7	4,723.5	9,714.8	8,882.5	4,090.5	31,293.0
Galvanized Iron	—	46.6	64.1	57.4	2.7	170.8
Total, All Material	3,956.5	4,926.5	10,056.5	9,355.4	4,174.7	32,469.6

2. Water Distribution Lines by Type of Material and Diameter

Material	*Size Range*	*Total in Place*	*Percent of Total*
Reinforced Concrete	36" to 84"	145.6	0.5
Steel	10" or less	5.6	
	12" to 30"	103.4	
	36" to 72"	751.1	
	Sub-total, Steel	860.1	2.5
Cast Iron	8" or less	17,801.3	
	10"	89.5	
	12" to 30"	12,561.2	
	36" to 48"	841.0	
	Sub-total, Cast Iron	31,293.0	96.5
Galvanized Iron	All Sizes	170.9	0.5
Total, All Materials	10" or less	17,896.4	
	12" to 30"	12,664.6	
	36" to 84"	1,737.7	
	Galvanized Iron	170.9	
	Total, All Sizes	32,469.6	100.0

SOURCE: *Annual Reports,* New York City Department of Environmental Protection (and predecessor agencies).

period in which various segments were developed. The following descriptive material on the city's sewer system by boroughs is based primarily on interviews with John DiMartino, Deputy Director of the Sewer Division in the Department of Environmental Protection.

Manhattan • The city's central borough is entirely sewered and virtually all of its lines are combined storm and sanitary sewers, initially constructed to discharge directly into the fast-flowing tidal rivers that surround the island. The tidal discharge design resulted in a gradual build-up of material in the sewers of Manhattan. As a result of the recent construction of a peripheral interceptor system to connect the borough's sewers to new water pollution control plants it is anticipated that much of this material will be removed by natural flows.

Manhattan sewers range in age from brick pipes built between the early 1830s and about 1920, plus a small number of sewers built since 1920 in the northernmost portions of the borough (Washington Heights). There were two peak periods of sewer-building: one in the 1830–40 decade and another in the 1870 to 1900 period. Most Manhattan sewers are egg-shaped (or oval) in cross-section. Common cross-sections are 2'4" by 3'2" and 3'2" by 4'0".

The complexity of underground systems in Manhattan and the enormous cost of reconstructing existing facilities has led to a city strategy of trying to retain and not replace the combined system of separate storm and sanitary sewers. This requires more waste water treatment capacity but is clearly a less costly approach than construction of a separate system.

Brooklyn • Most of Brooklyn is now sewered, almost all of it by combined storm and sanitary lines. There is a more modern, separated system at Coney Island.

Before the unification of Brooklyn with Manhattan at the end of the nineteenth century, a wide variety of different sewer systems were built in the independent localities of Brooklyn. The local systems in Brooklyn include some which were built to very poor standards. There is a critical problem, for example, in the Central Brooklyn-Williamsburg-Crown Heights area where the 75-year-old cement pipes are decomposing. Since 1960, the city has been replacing these defective pipes at the rate of 0.5 to 3 miles per day.

Queens • The borough with the largest area contains many of the city's most severe sewer problems. The historic development of Queens and also its topography led to the construction of a number of isolated sewer systems. As was the case in Brooklyn, some Queens communities (including Long Island City) were separate municipalities before the unification of the greater city and built their own systems.

Builders of extensive suburban developments in Queens from the 1930s to the 1950s tended to install sanitary sewers but not storm sewers; this was done because storm sewers are more costly and, in the builder's optimistic view, could be replaced by "natural" run-off to Jamaica Bay in the south or to Long Island Sound in the north. Perhaps the worst problem area for sewers in Queens is the Rockaway Peninsula, a low-lying sandy spit where substandard, leaky sewers result in flooding after even modest rainfalls.

The southern areas of Queens, which lack storm sewers, present a serious problem to the city. Not only will the installation be very costly but the grades necessary to assure adequate flow may result in sewer grades above the first floor levels of many existing dwellings.

Bronx • This borough presents less severe sewer problems than does Queens. Its system covers most of the borough (except for storm sewers in the northeast portions). South of Fordham Road, the artery which separates the south and north Bronx, the sewer system is combined and of reasonably adequate standards; portions that were reaching capacity have been relieved by a general exodus of population from the south Bronx. The housing north of Fordham Road is generally newer and of lower density than is that to the south, except for the modern, very high density Co-op City development.

Staten Island • As in the case of Queens, Staten Island is plagued by builder-constructed sewer systems without capacity to handle storm run-off in many of the built-up portions in the northern part of the island. Adequate storm sewers would leave many houses stranded below the grade level of the sewers.

The western shore of Staten Island is subject to severe flooding during high tides and heavy rains. A sea-front dike proposed by the Corps of Engineers to ward off hurricane-driven waves would, in the opinion of the city's Department of Environmental Protection, create an even more serious flood threat behind the dike.

Extensive areas in central and southern Staten Island are as yet undeveloped. They are laid out in a grid pattern that is very poorly adapted to either the hilly topography or proper drainage; as a result, a lack of sewers has been a major obstacle to development.

Overall, New York City is estimated to lack adequate sewerage in about 1,500 miles or 25 percent of its total street length. In addition, an estimated 40 percent of the existing system is more than 60 years old.

HIGHWAYS AND BRIDGES

The city's Department of Transportation does not maintain a street index or any other comprehensive file of data on the city's 6,000 miles of paved streets and highways. Thus, there are no consistent data available on the age or condition of the city's street system. In part, this situation is the result of the relatively recent centralization of highway responsibilities under the mayor's authority; before 1965, each of the five borough presidents had responsibility for streets within his borough.

Overall, the city's Department of Transportation estimates that there are 24,000 lane-miles of city streets plus 1,400 lane-miles of arterial highways.

New York City's system of bridges and tunnels includes a total of 1,337 structures so classified by the city's Department of Transportation.* Of the total, 775 are under the jurisdiction of various city agencies while the remaining 562 are classified as under state jurisdiction.

Structures under city jurisdiction include:

- 245 arterial highway structures
- 330 Transit Authority and railroad structures
- 144 park and street structures
- 51 waterway bridges
- 5 tunnels

The state jurisdiction structures are all part of the arterial highway system.

Figure 6 shows the location of the significant waterway bridges. It graphically depicts the complex problem created for the surface transportation system by the numerous waterways that divide the land mass of the city.

---

* *1977 Annual Report on Condition of Bridges and Tunnels*, New York City Department of Transportation.

FIGURE 6.

LOCATION OF WATERWAY BRIDGES, CITY OF NEW YORK

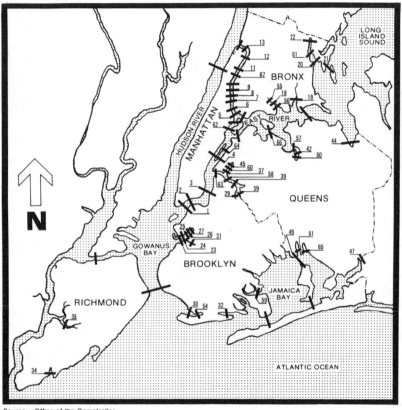

Source: Office of the Comptroller

Table 12

SELECTED CHARACTERISTICS OF THE NEW YORK CITY
RAPID TRANSIT SYSTEM COMPARED WITH THOSE
OF OTHER MAJOR CITIES, 1976

	Route-miles					Passengers (millions/ year)
City	Subway	Other	Total	Stations	Cars	
New York[a]	137.1	93.6	230.6	461	6,681	1,100
London	99.0	139.0	238.0	248	4,368	644
Paris	102.6	6.3	108.9	345	3,372	1,097
Tokyo	79.3	15.8	95.1	146	1,710	1,613
Moscow	81.2	11.2	92.4	96	1,800	1,841
Chicago	10.6	78.3	88.9	154	1,099	104
San Francisco[b]	19.3	55.9	75.2	34	450	7
Philadelphia	19.2	19.8	39.0	65	565	112

[a] Does not include Staten Island or PATH systems.
[b] Not based on full system operation.
SOURCE: "New York City Transit Facts and Figures, 1976," Public Affairs Department, New York City Transit Authority.

TRANSIT

New York City's subway system originated with a series of private companies that first developed elevated railways and then the subway lines. Before these systems were constructed, New York, in common with other older Eastern cities, had extensive networks of horsedrawn trams (the city's earliest started operation in 1827) and electric street cars. The first elevated train ran on Greenwich Street, Manhattan, in 1867. New York's East Side IRT line, now about to celebrate its 75th anniversary, is one of the nation's oldest subways.

Table 12 presents a comparison of New York's rapid transit system with the largest systems in other cities in the world and in the nation. Of the other urban rapid transit systems, only London's compares with New York's in extent, although the less extensive Moscow and Tokyo systems surpass it in ridership. No other American city has a system that is even close to New York's in terms of any of the criteria listed in the table.

Table 13 presents more detailed data on the tracks and roadways in the New York subway system. The extensive distribution of the system's lines throughout the city is shown on the accompanying map

Table 13

SELECTED CHARACTERISTICS OF TRACKS AND ROAD-
WAYS IN THE NEW YORK CITY RAPID TRANSIT
SYSTEM, 1976

1. By Type of Roadway

Type	Route-Miles		Track-Miles	
	Number	Percent	Number	Percent
Underground	137.1	59.5	448.5	63.3
Elevated	70.8	30.7	184.7	26.1
Other (open cut, embankment, surface)	22.8	9.9	75.4	10.6
TOTAL	230.6	100.0	708.6[a]	100.0

2. By Borough

Borough	Route-Miles		Track-Miles	
	Number	Percent	Number	Percent
Manhattan	71.1	30.8	224.0	31.6
Bronx	32.8	14.2	97.5	13.8
Brooklyn	84.1	36.5	260.5	36.8
Queens	42.7	18.5	126.6	17.9
TOTAL	230.6	100.0	708.6	100.0

[a] Does not include 120.1 miles of yard and storage tracks.

SOURCE: "New York City Transit Facts and Figures, 1976," Public Affairs Department, New York City Transit Authority.

(figure 7). The map also portrays the division of the system into
underground, elevated, and "at-grade" components.

The system is served by 197 electrical substations, which provide
the direct electric current needed for train operation by converting
alternating current. One-fifth of the substations were built prior to
1910 and half were built in the 1911–50 period. Since 1970, an extensive program of modernization has been renovating the older substations (25 modernizations have been completed).

The 458 passenger stations in the New York system are concentrated in Manhattan (138) and Brooklyn (171). Nearly three-fifths
of the stations are underground; most of the remainder are on the
elevated portions of the system; and less than 10 percent of the sta-

FIGURE 7.
RAPID TRANSIT SYSTEM LINE STRUCTURE CHARACTERISTICS

————————— SUBWAY
━━━━━━━━━ ELEVATED
▬▬▬▬▬▬▬▬ AT GRADE, OPEN CUT, OR EMBANKMENT

Source: A New Direction in Transit. Department of City Planning.

tions are at grade. Unfortunately, the 458 stations are served by a total of only 144 escalators and 23 passenger elevators.

Stations range widely in size, design, and use. Grand Central is the busiest with 29.8 million passengers in 1976, followed by 34th Street (at Avenue of the Americas) and Times Square with 23.4 and 22.3 million passengers each in that year.

The city's 6,681 subway cars comprise by far the world's largest fleet of such vehicles, a third larger than London's. Nearly one-third of the fleet is composed of quite new cars with stainless steel exteriors and over 2,000 are now air-conditioned. The subway car fleet has gone through several significant changes in recent years as major new purchases were made of 75-foot long vehicles for the IND and BMT systems (in contrast to the earlier 60-foot vehicles on these lines and the 51-foot cars on the older, more constricted IRT Division). There are roughly twice as many passenger cars on the IND/BMT Division as there are on the IRT (4,320, compared to 2,354 in 1976). The fleet total also includes 405 work cars such as locomotives, flatcars, cranes, revenue collection vehicles, and rubbish collection vehicles. The fleet has been replaced regularly on about a 35-year cycle.

The Transit Authority operates an extensive system of track and vehicle maintenance including 13 shops of which the largest are at Coney Island in Brooklyn and at 207th Street in Manhattan. Power for the system is purchased primarily from the New York State Power Authority and is distributed by the Consolidated Edison Company. As mentioned above, the Transit Authority purchases alternating current, which is converted to the direct current needed for train operation at 179 substations. About two billion kilowatt-hours annually are required to operate the system.

The Transit Authority also operates an extensive surface bus system, both directly and through its operating subsidiary, the Manhattan and Bronx Surface Transportation Operating Authority, the former Fifth Avenue bus line. Other bus systems in the city are operated privately. Table 14 summarizes key characteristics of the municipal bus system whose more than 4,500 buses make up the great majority of all such passenger vehicles in the city.

The bus system also requires an extensive garage and maintenance system. The largest shops are in the East New York district of Brooklyn and at 132nd Street in Manhattan. There are also 20 other combined maintenance depots and garages.

Table 14

SELECTED CHARACTERISTICS OF THE TRANSIT
AUTHORITY SURFACE TRANSPORTATION SYSTEM, 1976

Item	Transit Authority	MaBSTOA	Total
1. Buses (number)	2,540	2,040	4,580
2. Passengers (000's)			
Average weekday	1,009	975	1,984
Annual total	372,621	310,613	683,233
3. Scheduled trips (weekdays)	37,891	25,570	63,551
4. Bus miles traveled (000's)			
Regular	67,453	43,898	111,351
Express	4,239	1,455	5,694

SOURCE: "New York City Transit Facts and Figures, 1976," Public Affairs Department, New York City Transit Authority.

Condition of the Infrastructure: Selected Components

Given the absence of a physical inventory of New York City's public property in any consistent form, each agency accumulates information on its own area of responsibility, but much of it consists of the personal knowledge of agency staff members rather than comprehensive recorded data and measurements. The closest approximation to a central "data bank" on infrastructure condition is probably the collective knowledge of the engineering staff in the city Office of Management and Budget and the borough office staffs of the Department of City Planning.

Anecdotal evidence abounds, usually in the form of scare stories in newspapers or on TV news. While these serve a generally useful purpose by making the public—and public officials—aware of problem conditions, they do not provide anything like the consistent base of data that is necessary for program analysis and planning. The closing and collapse of the West Side elevated highway (built in the early 1930s and now being torn down in the 1970's) has become perhaps the archtypical instance of urban infrastructure deterioration. The dead highway is highly visible and its demise has created serious traffic problems in the city. What is unclear is the degree to which shortcomings in the original design contributed to the problems that afflicted the roadway and how many of the problems could have been avoided by good maintenance; patently, both were contributing causes. Much older elevated structures which are part of the city's transit system and which receive a higher level of continuing inspec-

tion and upkeep are apparently not in serious danger of following
the West Side highway into collapse in the near future.*

The sections which follow focus on four selected infrastructure
components (water, sewers, highways, and transit) and attempt to
assess their condition on the basis of four pertinent sources of
information:

- Direct measures of condition, in the few instances where
  these are available.

- Breakdown rates, as evidenced either by reported problems or
  responses to emergency situations.

- Replacement and rehabilitation rates, generally as evidenced
  by the physical amount of construction that has been put in
  place in recent years. (Planned replacement or construction
  rates are discussed in part III.)

- In the absence of hard data, subjective qualitative descriptions have been used in an effort to complete the picture of
  physical condition. To the degree possible, these assessments
  have been based on and/or calibrated against the judgments
  of knowledgeable observers of the city's infrastructure.

WATER SUPPLY AND DISTRIBUTION

Water Supply • The upstate reservoir and watershed system,
despite its age, is apparently in reasonably sound physical condition.
The most serious problems that confront the system are an apparent
inadequacy in the assured supply level in the event of an extended
drought and the possibility that a significant element of the system
(the Croton watershed) may be forced into filtration because of
encroaching urban development.

Water Distribution • The water distribution system below
Hillview reservoir is best viewed as two components: the three water
tunnels, and the system of mains that branches out from them.

The most troublesome thing about the two older water tunnels
is that little is known about their condition and, pending completion

---

* As indicated by a detailed inspection of the aged elevated transit structure in
Jamaica, Queens, described in "Elevated Lines Structural Survey Phase II Report"
prepared for the New York City Transit Authority by Ammann and Whitney,
Consulting Engineers, September, 1978 (mimeo).

of the stalled Third City Water Tunnel, neither can be closed down for inspection and repair. The city's engineers are afraid to use the by-pass sections put in place decades ago to allow inspection and repair because they might stick in a closed position, effectively closing off one of the existing tunnels. Completion of the Third City Water Tunnel, despite the substantial work done on it already, appears to be years in the future. The city's four-year capital program allocates only enough money to prevent deterioration of work in place, not for any forward movement. Under these conditions, the dangerous threat of a serious disruption in water service continues to loom over the city if either old tunnel becomes obstructed.

The remainder of the water system appears to be in reasonably good physical condition despite the growing age of many of its mains. Table 15 lists the number of breaks in the distribution system by major size categories of pipe; figure 8 shows the same data graphically.

Table 15

WATER MAIN BREAKS BY SIZE CATEGORY AND YEAR, 1966–76

	Size of Main (inches)			
Fiscal Year	*Under 12*	*12 to 35*	*36 and over*	*Total*
1978	NA	NA	NA	469
1977	NA	NA	NA	521
1976	375	99	9	483
1975	312	116	3	431
1974	341	120	8	473
1973	368	124	2	494
1972[a]	406	127	14	547
1971[a]	365	97	7	469
1970[a]	332	121	7	460
1969[a]	318	102	5	415
1968[a]	365	96	9	470
1967[a]	296	76	8	380
1966[a]	282	82	14	378

[a] The 1973 report says: "Years 1961 through 1972 included steel mains as breaks, but they were actually electrolysis leaks." It does not seem likely that this accounted for many of the breaks listed because cast iron pipes dominate the system.

SOURCE: *Annual Reports*, New York City Department of Water Resources, 1966–76 (table 5).

FIGURE 8.
WATER MAIN BREAKS, NEW YORK CITY,
FISCAL YEARS 1966-1976.

SIZE OF MAIN: UNDER 12 INCHES IN DIAMETER

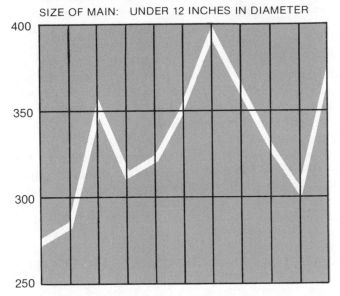

SIZE OF MAIN: 12 TO 35 INCHES IN DIAMETER

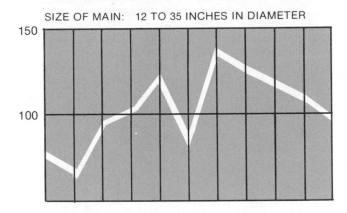

SIZE OF MAIN: 36 INCHES AND OVER IN DIAMETER

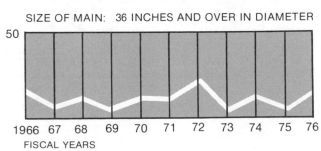

1966 67   68   69   70   71   72   73   74   75   76
FISCAL YEARS

The Department of Environmental Protection classifies a "break" as an actual disruption or separation in the material, in contrast to the less serious "leaks," which normally take place at joints. As can be seen from the table and the graph, there is no clearly discernible pattern of increase *or* decrease over time in the number of breaks, either for the whole system or for any of the size classes shown.

The total number of breaks per year remained in the range of 350 to 550 throughout the period covered in the table and, for most years, it ran a little above or below 450 total breaks. Nor did the distribution pattern show much change by size of pipe that broke. One-third to one-fourth of the breaks were in the size class 12 to 35 inches; very few (under 1 percent) were over 36 inches; and the rest were all small lines (under 12 inches). The latter are also the oldest in the system, by and large.

When the pattern of breaks is viewed over a longer period of time, there does appear to be a generally increasing number per year. From 1947 to 1976, the number of breaks rose from 234 to 483, more than doubling over a 29 year period.

However, it is not clear on the basis of available data, whether breaks are closely related to age of pipe. For example a 1977 study by a mayoral committee found that water pipes installed prior to 1870 failed less often than those installed from 1870 to 1889 and only slightly more often than those installed between 1890 and 1899. Pipes installed after 1900 did have a much better performance record.*

On the basis of this evidence, recent media reports of such spectacles as a 72-inch main break at the corner of Lexington Avenue and 42nd Street in Manhattan—flooding one of the city's busiest intersections for over a day—should be viewed as an unusual incident and not necessarily a trend indicator.

The construction program for water distribution since 1966 is summarized in table 16. It exhibits a very steady pattern. With only one exception (1974) the construction program involved installation of 40 to 60 miles of new mains and the removal of 20 to 40 miles of old mains, for a net gain of 20 to 40 (average 29) miles per year in the extent of the system. This steady pattern involved replacement of only about 30 miles of existing lines per year or about 0.5 percent

---

* Mayor's Select Committee on Water Main Breaks, cited in Office of the State Comptroller, Office of the Special Deputy Comptroller for New York City, "Some Effects of Deferred Maintenance of New York City's Water Distribution System As of November 1977" (memorandum dated March 12, 1979).

Table 16

WATER MAINS LAID AND REMOVED, 1966–76

1. Mains Laid, Removed and in Place (in miles)

Fiscal Year	Water Mains Laid	Water Mains Removed	Total Length in Place in December
1976	47.3	31.8	6,149.7
1975	51.0	40.9	6,134.2
1974	163.2	21.7	6,124.4
1973	41.2	24.7	5,982.7
1972	41.2	19.5	5,966.2
1971	40.8	21.5	5,944.6
1970	38.8	21.3	5,925.3
1969	40.3	18.5	5,907.7
1968	60.2	31.8	5,886.0
1967	58.7	33.8	5,857.5
1966	61.5	37.6	5,832.7
Total, 1966–76	644.2	303.1	N/A

2. Mains Laid and Removed as a Percentage of the Size of the System

Fiscal Year	Water Mains Laid	Water Mains Removed
1976	0.769	0.517
1971	0.687	0.361
1966	1.055	0.645

Source: *Annual Reports*, New York City Department of Water Resources, 1966–76 (table 9).

of the system. Thus, the implied replacement rate is about a 200-year cycle for the over 6,000-mile system.

Data on the installation and removal of hydrants and valves are shown in table 17. There was some change in the eleven-year pattern here, starting in 1974 when the rate at which new valves and hydrants were installed rose sharply. In that year, the installation rate more than doubled any preceding year, then dropped back in 1975 and 1976 to levels only about 50 percent above the pre-1974 period.

Interviews with Thomas O'Connell, Chief Engineer of the Water Resources Division of the Department of Environmental Protection, suggested that the level of concern over the need to invest more heavily in the water distribution system was higher than is

Table 17

VALVES AND HYDRANTS INSTALLED
AND REMOVED, 1966–76

Fiscal Year	VALVES			HYDRANTS		
	Installed	Removed	In Place	Installed	Removed	In Place
1976	1,922	1,099	176,637	1,371	1,136	93,826
1975	1,867	1,279	175,814	1,364	1,167	93,591
1974	4,202	674	175,226	2,480	531	93,394
1973	1,125	588	171,698	950	704	91,445
1972	1,091	470	171,162	492	196	91,199
1971	1,123	394	170,491	680	312	90,903
1970	1,119	522	169,835	604	349	90,535
1969	1,159	508	169,238	637	173	90,280
1968	1,548	645	168,586	590	172	89,929
1967	1,513	707	167,684	583	188	89,511
1966	1,698	720	166,878	707	278	88,116
Total 1966–76	18,367	7,606	N/A	10,458	5,206	N/A

SOURCE: *Annual Reports,* New York City Department of Water Resources, 1966–76 (table 10).

suggested by the data presented in this section. His concerns focused on the serious and complex problem of the Third City Tunnel, the difficulties of continuing to respond promptly and effectively to water main breaks with less manpower each year, and difficult-to-gauge anticipation that an increasing pattern of breaks could occur at any time in the aging system. These are all legitimate and serious concerns; they are relieved in some measure by his realization that the water distribution system has been given a high level of priority in the city's future capital program planning.

SEWERS

As already noted, the data for the sewer system are significantly less comprehensive than that for water. However, the sewer engineers are able to use one form of inspection that is not generally available for water lines: because pipes involved are generally large (especially in combined and storm sewers), newly developed TV techniques can be used for direct physical inspection of the condition of sewers. In many cases, this can be supplemented by visual inspection without TV.

In the absence of any comprehensive data base on the deterioration in the sewer system, it is at least suggestive to consider data from a monthly report presented by the Division of Sewer Maintenance at a departmental management review meeting. The monthly report noted receipt of 7,860 sewer-connected complaints in August, 1976, up 70 percent from the previous month (apparently because of heavy rains). Subtracting duplicate complaints about the same condition left 6,200 new complaints on top of a backlog of 1,081 unresolved complaints from the preceding month. The Division reported that it resolved 84 percent of the combined total of backlog and new complaints during August, leaving a backlog of 1,155 complaints as September began.

Most complaints fell into two categories in about equal proportions: sewer backups and catch basin clogging, both of which can

Table 18

CONSTRUCTION OF SEWERS, FISCAL YEARS 1965–79

Fiscal Year	Construction (Miles)	Construction Contract Awards ($ Millions)
1979	17.0 (plan)	N/A
1978	20.2 (est.)	41.0
1977	14.6	24.0
1976	17.0	7.3
1975	N/A	36.6
1974	N/A	30.4
1973	N/A	60.8
1972	60	31.7
1971	51	48.7
1970	33	23.6
1969	43	16.4
1968	34	7.9
1967	18	9.4
1966	19	6.9
1965	19	7.4

SOURCES: New York City Master Plan for New Sewer Construction, Management Plan Reports and Director of Construction.

generally be resolved through minor maintenance activities and involve no repairs or construction. Less than 10 percent of the complaints involved damaged or missing castings which require repair or construction. The division reported 153 repairs completed during August.

Construction data on the city's sewer system are shown in table 18. The record shows a pick-up in the rate of construction in the late 1960s and early 1970s as the Lindsay administration expanded the entire municipal construction program and the city for the first time began to address seriously the issue of its "missing" 1,500 miles of sewers. The fiscal crisis brought the sewer construction program to a virtual stop. Projects financed by Federal Public Works grants account for most of the sewer project starts in fiscal years 1977 and 1978.

HIGHWAYS AND BRIDGES

Highways • There are no consistent data available on the condition of the city's streets, although it is obvious to citizens and highway engineers alike that there are serious problems in road surfacing and drainage throughout the five boroughs. One report esti-

Table 19

SELECTED INDICATORS OF MAINTENANCE AND REPAIR, STREETS AND HIGHWAYS

	Fiscal Year					
Indicator	*1973*	*1974*	*1975*	*1976*	*1977*	*1978*
Potholes Filled (000's)						
Hot patch	899	973	670	548	605	N/A
Cold patch	331	373	247	501	210	N/A
Total filled	1,230	1,346	917	1,049	815	1,183
Sidewalks Installed						
(000's of square feet)	152	191	184	212	N/A	N/A

Sources: Management Control Reports (1973) and Management Plan Reports (1974 to 1978), New York City Department of Transportation.

FIGURE 9.
HIGHWAY RESURFACING, 1973-1978.

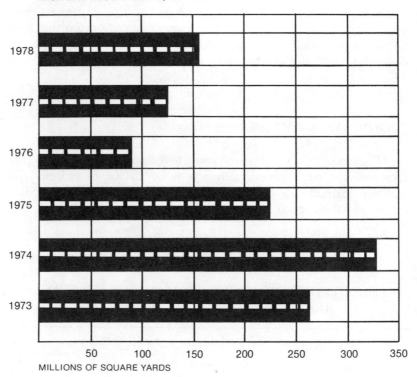

MILLIONS OF SQUARE YARDS

Source: New York City Department of Transportation
and Executive Budget Message, FY 1979.

mates a backlog of 2,300 miles (or about one-third of the total) that need complete reconstruction, not mere resurfacing.*

Several indirect measures indicate the magnitude of the problems: the Office of the Comptroller annually pays claims on the order of $10 million to persons injured because of faulty sidewalks or street surfaces; and each year the city fills on the order of one million potholes, or about one for every 30 feet of roadway (see table 19).

Figure 9 presents data on the rate at which the city is reconstructing and resurfacing its roadways. Over the six years from 1973 to 1978 inclusive, the peak year for resurfacing was 1974 when over 300 million square yards were paved; if that rate could be achieved each year, the average street would be resurfaced only about every 18 years. Reconstruction has rarely exceeded 40 miles of roadway per year or an implied rebuilding cycle for the entire system of once every century and a half. Patently, these rates are far too infrequent for the severe beating that most city streets take from traffic and the weather. City highway engineers believe that reconstruction should be undertaken every 25 to 40 years, depending on the level of traffic to which the street is subjected and on the fact that resurfacing *may* last only five years.*

Bridges • A number of the city's bridges and highway structures are in severe need of repair, primarily because of the lack of regular maintenance. A recent report by the city comptroller notes, "The city has virtually no program for the systematic maintenance of its bridges and arterial structures."**

The Department of Transportation maintains that under its inspection program it examines each of the 1,322 bridges and tunnel structures in the city once every two years, with more frequent attention given to the major East River crossings such as the Brooklyn and Manhattan Bridges and the operating drawbridges and tunnels. The results of a 1977 inspection are summarized in table 20.

One out of every ten bridge and tunnel structures was found to be in poor condition (defined as needing major reconstruction or replacement). Another 13 percent were assessed as being in fair condition (needing modernization or rehabilitation). The 133 structures found to be in poor condition fell into the following categories:

---

* *Civil Engineering Magazine*, November, 1978 (p. 73).

** *An Operational Audit of New York City Bridges and Arterial Structures*, Office of the Comptroller, City of New York, July 13, 1976 (mimeo).

Table 20

CONDITION OF BRIDGES AND TUNNELS
BY SELECTED CATEGORIES, 1977

By Number of Structures

| | Condition | | | | |
Type of Structure	Poor	Fair	Good	Very Good	Total
Arterial: City Jurisdiction	34	24	79	106	245
Arterial: State Jurisdiction	9	39	89	425	562
Off-System (Transit, Railroad, Street and Park) Structures	75	88	223	88	474
Waterway Bridges	13	17	10	11	51
TOTAL, All Structures	133	168	401	630	1332

By Percentage of Each Type of Structure

| | Condition | | | | |
Type of Structure	Poor	Fair	Good	Very Good	Total
Arterial: City Jurisdiction	15	10	32	43	100
Arterial: State Jurisdiction	2	7	16	75	100
Off-System (Transit, Railroad, Street and Park) Structures	15	19	47	19	100
Waterway Bridges	25	33	20	22	100
TOTAL, All Structures	10	13	30	47	100

SOURCE: 1977 Annual Condition Report of Bridges and Tunnels Under the Jurisdiction of the New York City Department of Transportation (March, 1978).

- 44 arterial highway structures (of which 36 were under city jurisdiction and 9 were under state jurisdiction)
- 65 transit and railroad structures
- 10 street or park structures
- 13 waterway bridges

Conditions appear to be worst in the waterway bridge category where one in every four structures was stated to be in "poor" condition and over one in two was found to be in less than "good" condition. Arterial structures listed as under state jurisdiction are apparently in significantly better condition than those under city jurisdiction; this is likely to be due to their more recent construction rather than to the amount of maintenance, since all maintenance work is done by city forces.

The city tries to paint its bridges every ten years but does not consistently meet this schedule (by its own admission). Bridge painting is done partly by in-house staffs and partly by outside contractors. As noted in part I of this report, the number of in-house painter-days available for structural maintenance fell by one-fourth from 1974 to 1978. This is apparently due, at least in part, to using the small staff of bridge painters for other, less urgent tasks.*

TRANSIT

The New York City Transit Authority's engineering staff estimates the overall value of the fixed rail system and the rolling stock as being on the order of $27 billion. If the system were being replaced on a 100 year cycle—which they believe is a plausible figure for the fixed plant but not the rolling stock—an annual investment on the order of $270 million would be required. They contrast this with their estimates that about $150 million per year has been invested in recent years (not counting construction of new lines) to indicate the general need for a higher level of investment.

It is difficult to assess the condition of the tremendously complex fixed plant and rolling stock system operated by the Transit Authority. There are, however, a variety of subsystems that transit staffs use to guide their maintenance and rehabilitation program. For example:

- The signal division maintains a computerized recording system based on monthly inspections of equipment under its jurisdiction. In a recent study,** the city's Department of City Planning notes that signal replacement is on a 45 year cycle, and that greatest emphasis is placed on the IRT division which contains the oldest signal installations.

- Tracks are examined by inspectors who walk the entire length of the system every 2.5 days.

---

* *An Operational Audit*, Office of the Comptroller, City of New York.
** *A New Direction in Transit*, New York City Department of City Planning (December, 1978).

- Three times a year the Sperry-Rand Corporation uses ultra-sonic techniques to test for breaks in rail or for defective welding.
- A special "geometry" car is run over the fixed rail system to test for alignment and profile.
- The Transit Authority attempts to maintain what it considers a minimally reasonable standard for key portions of equipment: 35 year replacement for subway cars; 15 years for buses; 40 years for signal systems and 35–40 years for escalators.

Principal attention in inspection and maintenance is given to safety; this has produced an excellent safety record, which is one of the Authority's most valued assets.

The subway car fleet appears to be in essentially sound condition, all of it being under the 35 year replacement target: its oldest cars were built 31 years ago, and with over 1,000 cars practically new (built since 1970).

There does appear to be a general correlation between the age of a subway car and its operating condition, based on the data presented in table 21 on miles of operation between breakdowns. The cars with the least miles of operation per breakdown were built in years ranging from 1948 to 1972 (most prior to 1957), while those with the most miles of operation without breakdown were generally newer, built in years from 1962 to 1978. Such factors as the degree to which cars have been reconditioned, the greater complexity of the more recently installed equipment, and other factors all contribute to the difficulties of interpreting these data. However, the overall pattern does appear to support the conclusion that the newer the car, the less likely it is to encounter operating difficulties.

Two recent engineering studies that were conducted by consultants to the Transit Authority provide insights into the condition of two of the most critical components of the fixed rail system: tracks and elevated structures.

A 1975 study of track maintenance* provided an overall picture of track conditions and suggested actions by the TA to develop a continuing system of assessment and improvement. The study found that fewer than 4 percent of train delays were attributable to track-related causes in the month of September, 1975. In the following

---

* *Track Maintenance Management Survey*, prepared by The Emerson Consultants for the New York City Transit Authority, November, 1975 (mimeo).

Table 21

DEPENDABILITY OF SUBWAY CARS
IN RELATION TO AGE

Car Designation	Miles/Breakdown (000's)	Year Constructed	Number of Cars
R–36	49.3	1964	424
R–32	31.3	1965	598
R–40	20.6	1967–8	199
R–46	19.2	1975–8	747
R–29	17.6	1962–3	236
R–42	17.6	1968–9	400
R–30	16.5	1961	317
R–38	16.0	1966	190
R–10	15.0	1948–9	389
R–26	14.1	1959–60	110
R–14	13.5	1949	139
R–33	12.6	1963	535
R–22	12.1	1957–8	446
R–27	12.1	1960	227
R–28	10.9	1960–1	100
R–17	10.7	1955–6	393
R–21	9.7	1956–7	249
R–12	9.6	1948	41
R–44	7.5	1971–2	300
R–16	5.7	1955	195

SOURCE: *A New Direction in Transit*, New York City Department of City Planning, December, 1978 (tables VI-1 and VI-2).

month the survey found that "slow speed" restrictions applied to only 2 percent of the entire system and that, of the 12 miles of track to which such restrictions applied, only 2 miles were due to track conditions. Derailments attributable to track-related causes have ranged from 7 to 15 per year over the last half dozen years.

In 1974, 63 track-miles of running rail were replaced, with an implied replacement cycle of about every 13 years. In the same year 71,000 ties were replaced with an implied replacement rate for the entire system of 35 years.

An outgrowth of the 1975 survey was the development by TA

staff of "work weighting" criteria to evaluate the need for track improvement. The approach assigns point scores to such conditions as:

- Potential disruption to service
- Type of service (local or express)
- Shape of tracks (curved or straight)
- Drainage conditions
- Rail conditions (wear, age, etc.)
- Condition of ties, tie plates and fastenings
- History of maintenance, delays, or track-walker complaints

A second engineering survey* focused on the condition of the Jamaica elevated structure. This facility is scheduled to be replaced at some point in the future (as have been many of the Authority's older elevated structures) but may have to last for another 10 to 15 years until that happens. The survey of this structure found that it was generally sound and well maintained but that there were some problems that needed detailed investigation and corrective action such as over-stressed beams and columns, corrosion in some through-girder areas, and some defects resulting from metal fatigue. The remaining life of the structure was estimated to be at least 15 years (or longer than it is expected to be in use). The engineers made a number of recommendations for corrective work and offered one reasonably conservative caution: that under wind conditions in excess of 65 miles per hour, traffic should be restricted (these are near-hurricane wind levels!).

Sway motion in the structure when trains pass over it were found to be very small: in the range of three- to five-sixteenths of an inch. Passengers feel this small sway as being greater, according to the engineers, because of the effect of train acceleration and deceleration.

The consulting engineers' basic recommendation—on which the TA has only just begun to follow up—was to carry out intensive examination of all of the remaining elevated structures which were built between 1885 and 1921. They noted that there is no basis currently available "for projecting future performance and durability of the structure." Conditions appear to be quite a bit better than those that affected the newer West Side Highway, in part because of

---

* "Elevated Lines Structural Survey Phase II Report," prepared for the New York City Transit Authority by Ammann and Whitney, Consulting Engineers, September, 1978 (mimeo).

higher TA maintenance standards and in part because the open design of the structures does not encourage corrosion by water or road salt.

Overall, the TA seems to have its maintenance program under reasonable control but staff members readily admit to a desire for much greater resources to maintain and replace aging components of the system. In addition, there are very worrisome problems due to a rising water table in parts of Brooklyn and Queens that may cause serious localized conditions.

SUMMING UP: CONDITION OF THE INFRASTRUCTURE

It is not at all easy to arrive at any comprehensive appraisal of the condition of New York City's infrastructure—or even the four major components that were the focus of this study—because of the enormous size, complexity, and variability of the systems involved. What does appear clear, at least to this writer, is the following:

- New York City is not "falling down"—to cite the refrain occurring in an otherwise excellent appraisal of the infrastructure presented on TV Channel 13, the city's principal noncommercial station. Its infrastructure *is* deteriorating and needs a significantly increased rate of investment in maintenance and replacement if serious problems are to be avoided in coming decades. It is a crisis that should be viewed in a perspective of years or decades—not days or months.

- The information base for realistic capital program planning and investment has serious shortcomings. These range from the lack of maps and inventories of facilities to the absence of consistent factual data on condition. Correcting these shortcomings would not be expensive in relation to the value of the capital investment already in place or the investments planned for the next four years; the failure to correct them may be costly indeed.

- Day-to-day maintenance may well be a more serious problem than investment in major rehabilitation or replacement of capital facilities. This problem is largely the consequence of the city's general fiscal problems. The city's expense budget (and that of the Transit Authority as well) is under very severe pressure and appears certain to remain so in coming years; it is this budget that provides financing for most maintenance activities. As will be reported in part III, the capital budget, which finances rehabilitation and reconstruction, now looms as a less serious problem—at least for the next four years.

Part III of this report examines the city's plans for investment in its infrastructure and tries to delineate the fiscal and other consequences that they imply.

Part 3
Future Trends and Prospects

Capital Planning
Since the
Fiscal Crisis

In 1977, at the depths of New York City's fiscal crisis, it was very difficult to foresee how the city might return to a level of capital construction that was even close to keeping pace with the deterioration of its infrastructure. In a report prepared for the Twentieth Century Fund that year, the author estimated the city's share of the capital program for the coming decade would have to be at least $10 billion, over and above any aid the city could reasonably expect from state or federal grants.* It was also estimated that overall needs from all funding sources would be over twice the amount appropriated in the preceding decade. In light of the difficult situation that existed in early 1977—the city's inability to sell bonds on the open market was only one of the serious obstacles to an expanded capital program—the report noted:

> In the absence of greatly expanded [state and federal] aid programs, New York City will be forced to make priority allocations of its scarce fiscal resources among the many desirable projects that could be undertaken. Among the first cutbacks in such a process are likely to be the investments necessary to maintain the quality of the water, street, and sewer systems.**

Fortunately, this anticipation appears to have proven unduly gloomy as to the city's fund-raising capacity, in large part because

---

* "Capital Construction Needs of New York City in the 1977–1986 Period," prepared for the Twentieth Century, New York, New York, Fund by David A. Grossman, February, 1977 (mimeo).
** Ibid., p. 88.

city and state officials began at about the same time to come to similar conclusions about the vital importance of an adequate capital program.

THE FINANCIAL PLAN OF 1978

In January, 1978, within days of taking office, the new administration of Mayor Edward I. Koch submitted a four year financial plan to the New York State Emergency Financial Control Board and the U.S. Treasury, setting forth estimates of the operating and capital budget needs of the city over the fiscal period 1979 to 1982 and explaining how the city proposed to deal with those needs. Among the components of the plan (whose preparation had begun in the closing days of the Beame administration) was a ten year capital plan estimating the city's construction requirements over the period 1978–88.*

The ten year capital plan, based partly on analyses presented in the earlier Twentieth Century Fund study, cited the serious need for investment in municipal physical plant and especially in infrastructure components. It set forth three principal objectives for the city's long-term capital program:**

- To establish and maintain realistic rehabilitation and maintenance schedules (including investments to address the serious past backlog of undone maintenance);
- To provide funds for capital projects to increase the revenue base of the city; and
- To provide funds for capital projects to reduce operating expenses.

Overall, the capital plan called for a ten year appropriation program of $12 billion for "brick and mortar" investment, plus additional funds for engineering staffs. Table 22 presents a summary of the city funds component of the ten year plan by major functional categories in terms of debt limit and exempt funds categories. Of those categories summarized in table 22, the four infrastructure systems selected for analysis here would account for two-thirds of the city's forecast needs over the decade:

---

* "Four Year Financial Plan for the City of New York" (New York City: Office of the Mayor, January 20, 1978) mimeo (section IV is the "Ten Year Capital Plan").
** Ibid., p. IV-2.

Selected Categories	FY 1979–88 ($ Millions)	Percent of Total
Water Supply and Distribution	$ 2,066	17.1
Water Pollution Control:		
Treatment Plants	218	1.8
Sewers	3,023	25.0
Highways and Bridges	2,376	19.7
Transit	205	1.7
Subtotal, Above Categories	7,888	65.3
Total, All Categories	$ 12,073	100.0

The greatly reduced share accounted for by transit—which has traditionally accounted for a much larger share of city capital spending—reflects the fact that the Office of Management and Budget expected state and federal aid (not included in the table) to finance the bulk of future transit construction in New York City. Similarly, OMB anticipated that future spending on treatment plants for water pollution control would also be supported substantially by state and federal grants.

THE FOUR YEAR PLAN AND FEDERAL GUARANTEES

The first four years of the ten year capital plan became the basis for the city's capital budget for fiscal 1979 and the capital program for the succeeding three years. In turn, this four year capital program became the cornerstone of the city's request to President Carter and the Congress for $2.4 billion in long-term federal loan guarantees to enable the city to sell its securities to its municipal employee pension funds if it were unable to raise funds elsewhere.

After extensive hearings by both houses of Congress, a compromise bill was passed and signed into law by President Carter in August, 1978, authorizing federal guarantees of up to $1.65 billion over the four year period. This legislative action was followed by an extended period of negotiation between city and Municipal Assistance Corporation officials, pension fund trustees, local banks and other financial institutions, and the Treasury. The result was in an agreement in November, 1978, under which the city's capital program will be financed during the fiscal 1979–82 period at a level of about $2.3 billion in long-term loans for the city's share of the program costs. (The plan at present calls for use of only $750 million in federal guarantees; additional use will require Treasury approval.)

It should be possible for the city to finance nearly the entire

Table 22

SUMMARY OF TEN YEAR CAPITAL NEEDS FORECAST
BY MAJOR FUNCTIONAL CATEGORIES,
FISCAL YEARS 1979 TO 1988
(City Funds for "Brick and Mortar" Only)

Category	Appropriations ($ millions)			
	Debt Limit Funds	Exempt Funds	Total City Funds	Percent of Total Appropriations
Economic Development	$ 496	—	$ 496	4.1
Education and City University	806	—	806	6.8
Pollution Control Plants	—	218	218	1.8
Sewers	977	2,046	3,023	25.5
Water Mains	—	959	959	8.1
Water Supply	—	1,107	1,107	9.3
Sanitation	458	—	458	3.9
Health and Hospitals	304	—	304	2.6
General Services	438	—	438	3.7
Museums and Institutions	28	—	28	0.2
Parks and Libraries	238	—	238	2.0
Correction	143	—	143	1.2
Fire	228	—	228	1.9
Police	133	—	133	1.1
Courts	131	—	131	1.1
Highways	1,890	—	1,890	15.9
Waterway Bridges	486	—	486	4.1
Traffic	37	—	37	0.3
Transit	205	—	205	1.7
Miscellaneous Other	402	125	527	4.4
TOTAL	$7,400	$4,455	$11,855	100.0

SOURCE: "Capital Budget Plan, 1979–1988" (New York City Office of Management and Budget, December 19, 1977) unpublished.

amount of its four year capital program within the overall level of borrowing authority that will be available even though the amount is substantially less than four-tenths of the estimated total cost of the ten-year program. There are two reasons for this.

First, the ten year plan calculations were based on reasonably realistic assumptions on how long it would take city agencies to do the necessary designing and planning to spur the construction program from near dormancy in early 1978 to a full-scale effort. Most of the phasing-in for an expanded scale of operation will occur during the first four years, so needs will be below average at the outset.

Second, the data contained in table 22, as well as the data in the city's fiscal 1979–82 Capital Budget and Program, are on the basis of appropriations, not on the basis of the actual cash that will be required to meet construction expenditures. In many cases there are time lags of two or more years between appropriation and cash outflow. The federal guarantees were approved in relation to actual cash needs, not appropriations.

PLANNING ASSUMPTIONS

In preparing its ten year capital plan the city's Office of Management and Budget developed estimates of investment rates that it believed were appropriate both (a) to cut into the backlog of undone repair work and investment in worn-out infrastructure components, and (b) to establish a sound "steady state" rate of investment. These are spelled out for each functional category in the plan itself.

In addition, OMB placed a somewhat artificial "ceiling" on its estimates of city capital expenditures in the years after fiscal 1984 for purposes of the financial plan (but not the capital plan itself). The financing ceiling was set at $1.2 billion from fiscal 1985 to 1988, in contrast to the "brick and mortar" appropriation needs shown in table 23 that rose from $1.3 to $1.5 billion over the period. In doing so, OMB stated its assumption that "the balance would be made available through such programs as Federal Public Works and Community Development."*

The capital program assumptions and associated cost estimates for each of the four infrastructure components analyzed here are presented in table 23 and are described below. In each case the Office of Management and Budget estimated escalation of construction costs at a rate of about 5 percent per year after the initial year: escalation data are shown separately in the table for each program.

---

* *Ten Year Capital Plan*, p. IV-5 (footnote).

Table 23

CAPITAL PROGRAM NEEDS IN WATER, SEWERS, HIGHWAYS, AND TRANSIT, FISCAL YEARS 1979–88
(in $ Millions)

Function/Element	Ten Year Total ($ Millions)	
1. Water		
a. *Water Mains*		
75 years replacement cycle (about 80 miles/year)	561	
Routine rehabilitation	29	
Upstate watershed rehabilitation	51	
Expansion of system (15 miles/year)	73	
Connections to 3rd City Tunnel	60	
Escalation	185	
Total		959
b. *Water Supply*		
Complete 3rd City Tunnel	943	
Escalation	164	
Total		1,107
2. Water Pollution Control		
a. *Treatment Plants*		
Renovation of existing plants	20	
Completion and/or upgrading of existing plants	198	
Total		218
b. *Sewers*		
New storm sewer (75 miles/year)	820	
New sanitary sewer (75 miles/year)	369	
Replace undersized sewers (50 miles/year)	614	
Replace worn-out sewers (60 miles/year)	738	
Escalation	481	
Total		3,022
3. Highways and Bridges		
a. *Highways*		
Crash effort to reconstruct worst roads in next twenty years	833	
Reconstruction on a 35 year cycle (3600 miles)	697	
Replace the busiest 2000 miles	60	
Escalation	300	
Total		1,890

Table 23—Continued

Function/Element	Ten Year Total ($ Millions)	
b. *Bridges*		
Five year crash effort on 1,000 bridges in worst need (200/year)	320	
Forty year cycle for remaining 1,000 bridges (50/year)	90	
Escalation	76	
Total		486
4. *Transit*		
Completion of new routes (subway) and on-going renovation	177	
Escalation	28	
Total		205

SOURCE: "Capital Budget Plan, 1977–1988," New York City Office of Management and Budget, December 19, 1977 (unpublished).

Water Distribution and Supply

(*Water Mains*) A long-term target replacement cycle of 75 years was assumed after an intensive five year effort at twice as fast a rate (starting in fiscal 1981 to allow lead time for design). Additional, lesser amounts were allocated for routine rehabilitation work in the distribution system and at the upstate reservoirs. For 1986–88, funds were allocated for trunk main connections to the Third City Water Tunnel.

(*Water Supply*) It was assumed that the Third City Water Tunnel's first stage would be completed during the decade at a somewhat artificial rate of $50 million per year for the initial two years, followed by about $100 million per year for the next eight years. In the actual capital budget for 1979 the amount appropriated was only $15 million, barely enough to maintain the unfinished construction in its present condition; similar amounts were included in each year of the three year capital program (1980–82).

Water Pollution Control

(*Treatment Plants*) The program would provide the city share of the remaining cost of treatment plant construction, plus about $2 million per year for renovation of portions of existing plants.

(*Storm Sewers*) A twenty year program to complete the city's storm sewer system was assumed at a rate of 75 miles per year with a ten year target of 1,500 miles of new sewers.

(*Sanitary Sewers*) It was also assumed that a comparable twenty year program for less costly sanitary sewers would complete the same 1,500 miles of needed work. In addition, a twenty year program to replace 1,000 miles of undersized sanitary sewers was assumed, together with replacement of 60 miles per year of existing, worn-out or defective sewers.

Highways and Bridges

(*Highways*) The program for highway improvement was divided into three parts: first, a "crash" program to rebuild the worst 40 percent of the city's 6,000 miles of highways over the next 20 years; second, replacement of another 3,500 miles of streets at a rate of 100 miles per year (a 40 year program); and third, a limited-objective program to replace the wearing surface of the city's busiest 2,000 miles of streets at a rate of 57 miles per year.

(*Bridges*) A two part program for 2,000 bridge structures was proposed consisting of, first, a "crash" program to address the needs of the structures in worst condition and, second, a forty year reconstruction cycle for all such structures.

Transit

A minimal program of city contribution to the transit capital program was assumed in OMB's capital plan. A total of $177 million was included, purportedly intended to complete the new routes now under construction and to fund the city matching share of renovation and modernization of the existing system. State and federal funds were presumed to constitute the bulk of transit investment.

An alternative—and considerably larger—estimate of transit construction needs over the next decade is available from another source. In July, 1977, the Metropolitan Transportation Authority (MTA) responded to a request by the Urban Mass Transportation Administration (UMTA) of the U.S. Department of Transportation for a ten year estimate of capital funding needs to upgrade and expand

the bus, subway, and commuter railroad facilities under its jurisdiction.*

A summary of the MTA plan for the capital needs of the subway system is contained in table 24. Major components of the plan
would be devoted to rehabilitation of the existing rail system: $3.9
billion or nearly 40 percent of the improvements were proposed for
the existing system.

The MTA forecast did not provide the proposed financing of its
program into city, state, and federal components; thus, it is not
possible to compare it directly to the OMB's ten year forecast of $177
million (not including escalation) for the city funds share of the
transit construction program. It does, however, seem unlikely that
even quite generous state and federal aid for transit could make it
possible to carry out the MTA's large-scale program with a city contribution of only 1.25 percent of the total.

AN ALTERNATIVE ESTIMATE OF TRANSIT NEEDS

In a recently published report,** the New York City Department
of City Planning has presented an alternative ten year forecast of
needs for investment in the transit system. The City Planning analysis
was largely derived from the MTA ten year capital needs program but
differs from it with respect to the overall size of the proposed program
and to the relatively high priority assigned to rehabilitation of existing system components.

Overall, the city planning alternative suggests a transit program
that is roughly half the size of MTA's needs estimate. This lower
level, the report notes, "is the result of eliminating less essential programs and finding less capital intensive alternatives" (page IV-7).

The City Planning study divided transit needs into five priority
categories:

- *Priority* A covered absolutely essential needs to maintain
  safety and reliability over the immediate future. Projects in
  this category were estimated to cost $200 million per year,
  slightly more than the average amount available over the last
  three years.

---

* "Metropolitan Transportation Authority Ten Year Capital Needs," The Metro-
politan Transportation Authority, July 30, 1977 (mimeo).
** *A New Direction in Transit*, New York City Department of City Planning
(December, 1978).

- *Priority B* would include projects to improve passenger comfort and also insure safety and reliability over the longer run. These were estimated to cost $140 million per year.
- *Priority C* included additional important projects that were estimated to cost $215 million per year.

Table 24

TEN YEAR CAPITAL IMPROVEMENT PROGRAM
FOR THE NEW YORK TRANSIT AUTHORITY,
1978–88

Item	Amounts ($ Millions)	
1. Rehabilitation of Existing Facilities		
Line Structures	$ 1,325	
Track	1,555	
Line Equipment	1,010	
Total		3,890
2. Purchase of New Vehicles		
Rapid Transit Cars	952	
Buses	585	
Total		1,537
3. Additional Items:		
Signals and Communications	515	
Power Equipment and Modernization	399	
Station Improvements	1,641	
Rehabilitation of Shops and Maintenance Facilities		
Rapid Transit System	475	
Bus System	428	
Emergency Equipment	326	
Special Facilities for Elderly and Handicapped	734	
Other		
Security Systems	67	
Agency Administration	40	
Service Vehicles	25	
Total		4,650
4. New Routes		4,025
GRAND TOTAL		$14,102

Source: "Metropolitan Transportation Authority Ten Year Capital Needs," Metropolitan Transportation Authority, July 30, 1977 (mimeo).

- *Priorities D and E* included nonessential projects that were not included in the recommendations. Their costs (which *were* included in the MTA needs forecast) would be on the order of $610 million per year.

On balance, the city planning revision of the MTA ten-year forecast appears to present a more realistic estimate—at least to this writer —than do either the apparently understated figures in OMB's ten year capital program or the very high estimate presented to UMTA by the MTA.

SOURCES OF FINANCING

With the approval of federal long-term guarantees and the negotiation of financing agreements with the Municipal Assistance Corporation, the banks, and employee pension funds, New York City appears reasonably assured of financing for the first four years of its ten year capital construction plan. The subsequent years of the program remain in question pending the resolution of such major issues as:

- Whether the city will be able to return to the municipal security market after 1982 and sell long-term bonds in amounts on the order of $1.2 billion per year as called for in its plan. (As noted, this would still fall about $300 million per year short of forecast capital expenditures.)
- If the city proves unable to return to the market, the issue of additional federal guarantees will arise; it is still far too early to estimate whether this would prove politically feasible.
- The plan assumes a continuation of current types of state and federal aid over the decade (concentrated in transit and water pollution control) but is not based on any major new types of capital aid.

The $1.2 billion per year level is not sharply different from security sales levels the city reached during the period before the fiscal crisis. When the crisis arose, the problem appeared more focused on the rapidly rising levels of short-term notes the city was selling (which in 1974 accounted for a quarter of the national market of short-term municipal paper) rather than the long-term securities. Thus, the overall level may not constitute a problem in and of itself; the problem will be the general investor attitude toward municipal securities and those of New York City in particular.

THE FISCAL IMPACT OF THE CAPITAL PLAN

The city has prepared an analysis of the impact that its ten year capital construction plan will have on its budget and tax rate and the burden of anticipated real estate taxes on the economic base of the city.* The assumptions used in the estimates appear to be generally realistic, with three major exceptions:

- The analysis assumes that in the post-1982 period the city will be able to issue bonds in the necessary amounts with an average maturity of 23 years at an interest rate of 7.5 percent. Shorter maturities or higher interest rates would increase the annual debt service assumptions; for example, at an interest rate of 9 percent annual debt service costs would rise by about one-tenth by 1994. Shorter maturities could have an even greater effect.

- As noted above, the plan assumes that the city will be able to re-enter the securities market after 1982.

- The escalation figure of 5 percent may turn out to be too low.

One other assumption in the report is a continuation of recent patterns of growth in the taxable real property base of the city. One could argue with such an assumption as being either excessively optimistic or pessimistic; this writer concludes that, on balance, it is a realistic assumption in light of the differing trends exhibited within the city: declining values in the poverty neighborhoods such as the South Bronx and the apparent beginnings of a new boom in commercial and residential property in Manhattan.

Table 25 summarizes the results of the city's analysis in terms of two significant indicators: debt service as a fraction of the city's expense budget and as a fraction of total equalized (market) values for taxable real property.

New York City has traditionally borne a heavy level of debt service in comparison with many other municipalities. The forecast burden indicates a reduction from the burden during the fiscal crisis period (when debt service accounted for a third of the operating budget) to a longer-term level of about one-fourth; even this level, of course, is higher than the one-fifth level that characterized many years prior to 1965. Similarly, the forecast burden of debt service on the tax base suggests a return in the direction of the pre-crisis burden

---

* *Perspective on Debt and Debt Service*, FY 1960–1978, Office of the Deputy Mayor for Finance, New York City, December, 1977 (mimeo).

Table 25

DEBT SERVICE IN RELATION TO THE EXPENSE BUDGET AND EQUALIZED VALUE OF TAXABLE REAL PROPERTY, FISCAL YEARS 1960–90

Fiscal Year	Debt Service ($ Million)	Debt Service as a Percent of Expense Budget	Debt Service as a Percent Valuation of Equalized
1990 (est.)	2,240.0	N/A	1.86
1980 (est.)	1,955.0	24.4	2.13
1978 (est.)	2,067.0	25.2	2.40
1977	2,344.0	32.9	2.82
1976	2,310.4	35.3	2.84
1975	1,896.0	25.4	2.44
1970	767.6	19.1	1.27
1965	545.5	21.1	1.24
1960	418.0	23.0	1.47

NOTES: (1) 1980 and 1990 equalized valuation projected on basis of annual rate of increase 1975–1978.
(2) Debt service includes cost of both City and MAC short- and long-term debt.

SOURCES: *Perspective on Debt and Debt Service,* Office of the Deputy Mayor for Finance and Citizens Budget Commission (1960 equalization data).

of 1.25 to 1.5 percent of property values, but it will be nearly a decade before the burden goes below 2 percent. These debt service burden estimates indicate that if New York City is to support its ten year capital plan without substantial amounts of additional state and federal aid it will not only have to achieve a successful re-entry to the municipal security market but will also have to accept a higher burden of debt service that it was accustomed to in the pre-crisis period.

ASSESSING THE CITY'S PLAN

The capital program for the next ten years, which formed the basis for the city's successful request for long-term federal guarantees, sets ambitious construction targets, even in relation to the city's prior achievements in the booming 1970–75 period. It also represents a major refocusing of the city's own funding of its capital program from

Table 26

PRIOR AND PROPOSED APPROPRIATION OF CITY
CAPITAL FUNDS FOR SELECTED FUNCTIONS,
FISCAL DECADES 1969–78 AND 1979–88

	FY 1969–78		FY 1979–88 (est.)	
Function	$ Millions	Percent of Total	$ Millions	Percent of Total
Education (including CUNY)	1,996.9	23.0	806	6.8
Pollution Control Plants	629.8	7.2	218	1.8
Transit	1,185.8	13.6	205	1.7
Sub-total, above items	3,812.5	43.8	1,229	10.3
Water (Mains and Supply)	375.5	4.3	2,066	17.4
Sewers	509.8	5.9	3,023	25.5
Highways and Bridges	533.5	6.1	2,376	20.0
Sub-total, above items	1,418.8	16.3	7,465	62.9
Total, All City Funds	8,695.6	100.0	11,855	100.0

Sources: New York City Capital Budgets, 1969–78; Ten Year Capital Plan, 1979–88.

the past decade's concentration in education, transit, and pollution control plants to an emphasis in the next decade on the water, sewer, and street systems. This can be seen in table 26 which compares city funds appropriated and proposed for appropriation during the past and coming decades.

Nearly half of all city capital funds in the prior decade went to education, transit, and pollution control, with only about one-sixth invested in water, sewers, and the highway system. In the coming decade the education, transit, and pollution control appropriations are forecast to decline to one-tenth of total city funds, while the combination of water, sewers, and streets rises to more than three-fifths of all city capital funds.

It should be noted that the funds measured in table 26 are city funds only, *not* the total funds available for capital spending in the next decade from state and federal grants. While the city's ten year capital plan did not present estimates for anticipated intergovernmental aid, it seems clear it was framed on the assumption that such aid would continue to be concentrated in transit and water pollution control.

Even taking into account the potential for state and federal aid, however, the predicted shift in municipal spending priorities may prove, in practice, to be difficult to accomplish because of both political and planning problems. The education program, in particular, retains strong political influence in the Board of Estimate and City Council and may well account for a larger share of city funds than forecast in the ten year plan even in the face of continually declining enrollments. The forecast for transit also seems quite low in comparison with past appropriations even if the city continues to receive large amounts of federal and state aid in this area. On the other hand, much as the increased emphasis proposed for the basic infrastructure components of water, sewers, and streets may be justified by need, the disruption of neighborhood life implied by the massive construction targets may prove to be a very real constraint on the pace of such construction. For example, neighborhoods for which new sewer and street systems are proposed often find—to their dismay—that the new street grades will be six to ten feet above present street levels, leaving their houses well below street level. In such cases, the demand for an end to flooding and decomposed roadways tends to decline in the face of the realization of what new construction will mean to living conditions.

As already noted, it is impossible to forecast whether the city will actually be able to obtain the financing needed for the proposed capital program. One important determinant of this issue is likely to be the future pattern of federal and state aid. Of the three "emphasis" programs planned by the city for the next decade, only the street system now benefits from more than miniscule amounts of aid. Progress on the water and sewer systems may well prove dependent on whether intergovernmental aid becomes available for such activities in the future. In recognition of this, the city has already begun discussing financing of the Third Water Tunnel with federal agencies.

It does not appear likely that New York City will change its prior pattern of using federal general revenue sharing funds for operating (rather than capital) purposes; the continuing pressures on the city's expense budget are such as to make a shift from operating to capital expenditure highly unlikely. In addition, the city may be forced to use more of its Community Development block grant funds for capital purposes in future—not by its own choice—because federal regulations are becoming increasingly restrictive on the use of such funds for operating purposes except in specific, limited "neighborhood strategy areas."

The economic impact of the ten year program does not appear to be clearly beyond the city's capacity to afford, but the cost of accepting it is a near doubling of the long-term burden of debt service on taxable real property. And, if the interest rate and bond term assumptions in the city's forecast prove incorrect (as one suspects they may), the impact of debt service on city taxpayers could be sharply higher.

On the positive side, one significant benefit of the city's preliminary planning is that it begins to reveal the physical and financial implications of what it will take to overcome the increasing deterioration of the environment. The planning that has been done to date— as evidenced in OMB's unpublished "Ten Year Capital Plan" and the Deputy Mayor for Finance's "Perspective" report—is an important start on the type of long-range capital program planning that is essential. What is now needed is for the city to continue and intensify this planning process. Among the steps needed are (1) linking capital project planning to neighborhood-oriented land-use planning (a process that has only begun) and (2) considering what options may be available if either the predicted financing or physical programs prove impossible to put in operation in the precise form in which they have been projected.

Another related aspect of planning for infrastructure improvement is investment in day-to-day maintenance. As noted earlier in this report, little has as yet been done on this score and the expected pattern of continuing and severe pressure on the operating budget suggests that the problem is likely to get worse before it gets better.

Taken together, these needs for improved and intensified planning analysis—building on what appear to be sound initial foundations—present one of the most important agendas for New York City in the next few years. Fortunately, the four-year long-range financing plan that is now in place allows precisely the breathing room that is needed to permit city agencies to address this agenda.

THE ABILITY TO SPEND CAPITAL FUNDS

One final aspect of the city's future capital program that deserves mention may strike an observer as unusual, given the fiscal problems faced by New York City in recent years: there are significant obstacles that must be overcome before the city will be able to spend the capital funds made available through federal loan guarantees and the agreement by municipal employee pension fund trustees to purchase the city's bonds.

These difficulties arise partly from the fact that the fiscal crisis and the lack of capital funds in recent years resulted in a major slow-down in the capital project planning process. Engineering staffs as well as operating personnel were reduced by layoffs and attrition; the "pipeline" of plans in progress fell off sharply; and the management and information systems developed in the late 1960s to expedite capital construction deteriorated through lack of use. These problems must now be remedied. In addition, the new focus on underground infrastructure will require different approaches to the coordination of design and construction than did the city's previous emphasis on above-ground structures (such as schools and pollution control plants).

A rough measure of the difficulty of re-energizing the construction program can be seen from the successive lowering of city construction spending plans for fiscal 1979:

- The initial target for "brick and mortar" spending (exclusive of engineering design costs) for fiscal 1979 was set in the Financial Plan of January, 1978, at $348 million

- By the start of the fiscal year in July, 1978, the target for the year has been reduced to $317 million

- In September, 1978, the target was further reduced to $273 million

- By December, 1978, half-way through the fiscal year, the city submitted to the Financial Control Board an even lower target figure of $233 million

In fact, actual spending of city capital funds through December, 1978, reached a level of only $73 million, indicating that even the December target may be too high.

For New York City to achieve the capital construction targets set in its four and ten year programs may well require an overhaul of its current administrative structure supporting the design and construction of capital projects. This would include such features as:

- Revitalizing the critical path-based capital project information system that schedules and tracks capital projects. Since the fiscal crisis struck in 1975 this system has lost most of the staff that fed current data to the computerized system. Further, changes in the city charter in 1975 (for example, those providing major new roles in capital project review to

Community Boards and the Board of Estimate) have made obsolete the time schedules on which the computerized tracking system was based.

- Many city agencies have lost engineering design and review staff, who must be replaced.

- The city's procedures for award of engineering and architectural design contracts—always a major point of delay even in the best of times—must be overhauled and streamlined.

- The coordination of the complex construction process must be greatly strengthened so that projects do not compete in unplanned fashion for the scarce resources of design review staffs and contractors willing to work on city projects. This process involves a host of activities ranging from assuring equal opportunity for minority contractors and employees to expediting payment processes for vendors and contractors.

Improving the capacity of the city to plan and build capital projects will not be easy—but it is not by any means impossible as the city has demonstrated in the past. Without concentrated attention, however, it could well take another two years before New York City begins to approach the ambitious capital spending levels forecast in the financial plan for fiscal years 1979–82.